# Native America
# and the Evolution
# of Democracy

# Native America and the Evolution of Democracy

A Supplementary Bibliography

Compiled by
Bruce E. Johansen

Bibliographies and Indexes in American History, Number 40

Greenwood Press
Westport, Connecticut • London

**Library of Congress Cataloging-in-Publication Data**

Johansen, Bruce E. (Bruce Elliott), 1950–
    Native America and the evolution of democracy : a supplementary
bibliography / compiled by Bruce E. Johansen.
        p.  cm.—(Bibliographies and indexes in American history,
    ISSN 0742–6828 ; no. 40)
        Includes indexes.
        ISBN 0–313–31010–6 (alk. paper)
        1. Iroquois Indians—Politics and government—Bibliography.
    2. Indians of North America—Politics and government—Bibliography.
    3. United States—Civilization—Indian influences—Bibliography.
    4. United States—Politics and government—Bibliography. 5. United
    States—Historiography—Bibliography. I. Title. II. Series.
    Z1210.I7J63  1999
    [E99.I7]
    016.97304′9755—dc21          98–33136

British Library Cataloguing in Publication Data is available.

Library of Congress Catalog Card Number: 98–33136
ISBN: 0–313–31010–6
ISSN: 0742–6828

First published in 1999

Greenwood Press, 88 Post Road West, Westport, CT 06881
An imprint of Greenwood Publishing Group, Inc.

∞™

The paper used in this book complies with the
Permanent Paper Standard issued by the National
Information Standards Organization (Z39.48–1984).

10 9 8 7 6 5 4 3 2 1

# Contents

# Preface

*As to our aboriginal or Indian population...I know it seems to be agreed that they must gradually dwindle as time rolls on, and in a few generations more leave only a reminiscence, a blank. But I am not at all clear about that. As America...develops, adapts, entwines, faithfully identifies its own -- are we to see it cheerfully accepting using all the contributions of foreign lands from the whole outside globe -- and then rejecting the only ones distinctively its own? (Moquin, 5-6)*

**Walt Whitman, 1883**

Increased general awareness of Iroquois precedents for democracy (and the continuing debate over them) has not kept a rather sizable number of people (some of them conservatives bearing household names) from dismissing the idea with a spit and a sneer, with no knowledge that a genuine debate has been engaged. During the last few years, with a mixture of consternation and awe, I have watched a number of very well-known conservative authors and pundits attempt to turn the idea I have researched into canon fodder in the so-called culture wars over multicultural education. The idea of Iroquois influence (and the sharp debate over it) has spread out much faster than the research and understanding of historical circumstances required to make sense of it.

Having researched the question of Iroquois influence in the origins of democracy since the middle 1970s, I began an annotated bibliography of reactions to the idea during the early 1990s. In 1996, roughly the first 500 of these reactions were published by Greenwood Press as *Native American Political Systems and the Evolution of Democracy: An Annotated Bibliography.* By 1999, the number of reactions had reached 1,000. The second half of these are contained in this volume.

This is a subject that tempts the willingly ignorant to make rash statements. With mass media attention to the idea of Iroquois influence, the rhetoric of the debate has slipped its historical moorings and been driven into a rhetorical sea by contemporary storms over political correctness and multiculturalism. Ground up and spit out by the likes of Rush Limbaugh, *et a l.*, the "debate" becomes a muddy porridge of buzzwords and factoids, simplified, then blown horribly out of proportion to make the case for Iroquois influence sound ridiculous and vapid. The forging of historical memory on a mass scale can be a very strange process, indeed.

As a student of communication, I have assembled a referential history of the "influence" idea to illustrate how an idea can spread through literate culture at several levels. Aside from its ability to cause numerous well-known conservatives to lose their intellectual lunches, the "influence" idea has been adapted to debates in several academic fields, most often in law, American history and Native American Studies, but also in English, philosophy, religion, and public administration, along with sociology, anthropology, and ethnohistory.

The idea that the Iroquois helped shape democracy has lost none of its power to evoke horror stories of "political correctness" on the Far Right. Jonathan Foreman, in William F. Buckley's *National Review*, bemoans his belief that "Baby Boomers" have infected Hollywood movies with liberal values based on their "generational experience" in the 1960s. Collectively, Foreman argues, these "Boomers" are shaping the media with their "delusions." He moans, by way of letting his conservative audience know just how stupid the "Boomers" can be, that "We live in a society where some students are taught that the United States Constitution was inspired by the Iroquois, that the Greeks stole science from Africans, and that the Aztecs were sweeties who didn't really eat people like popcorn." (Foreman)

"We have already seen this in feminist and Afrocentric studies," writes Robert H. Bork, in his 1996 polemic *Slouching Toward Gomorrah: Modern Liberalism and American Decline*. "But it is everywhere. In New York State it is official educational doctrine that the United States Constitution was heavily influenced by the political arrangements of the Iroquois Confederacy." (Bork, 306-307)

Bork has made up his mind with the certitude of the supremely ignorant that research cannot possibly exist on such a silly subject as how the Iroquois Confederacy helped shape democracy. He writes, with an air of apparent authority: "The official promulgation of this idea was not due to any research that disclosed its truth," but because "the Iroquois had an intensive lobbying campaign." (Bork, 306-307)

There you have it in the Book of Bork -- "no research," and from a person who has been called a legal scholar, one who has been nominated to sit on the U.S. Supreme Court. Really, it is Bork who has done no research on the subject. One learns very quickly that in the marketplace of ideas some people have big bullhorns, and others have small ones. I have learned that my bullhorn as a scholar sometimes carries a very, very small toot. In the meantime, Bork's book reached the number eight slot on the *New York Times* list of best-selling non-fiction books in the United States.

Bork ends his diatribe against the issue by claiming that he speaks for the 38,000 Iroquois in New York State, "most of whom probably have no interest in the myth of the Iroquois and the Constitution" (Bork, 307). In one paragraph, Bork indicts the Iroquois for muscling the idea into the New York State educational system, and in another he says they really don't care. Bork supplies no Iroquois support for his assertion.

Bork's is merely one of the most hysterical of several recent reactions to a valid effort to broaden the ambit of our political history. Phyllis Schlafly, for example, grumbled in an opinion piece for the Copley News Service that, "A high school social studies teacher told me that three new social-studies textbooks all pay homage to the new gods of multiculturalism by teaching that we got our Constitution from the Iroquois Indians." (Schlafly)

I should not, of course, let Schlafly's reference to me as one of the "gods of multiculturalism" go to my head, since she (nor Bork) probably has never heard of (much less read) anything I have written on this or any other subject. I have followed the unfolding of this debate for a quarter century, and never cease to be amazed at the fact that I seem to have lucked onto a dissertation subject on which nearly everyone feels compelled to take a political position, including a sizable number of people who know very little about the subject. Count among them Rush Limbaugh, Patrick Buchanan, John Leo, and George Will, to name a sampling whose views appeared in the first bibliography.

Condemnation of the Iroquois-influence idea is not limited to generalists such as Limbaugh. Some of the scions of the American Society for Ethnohistory have been just as dismissive, although in a more elegant tone. Beginning with Elisabeth Tooker's 1988 critique of "influence," *Ethnohistory*, the society's journal, has long been a font of anti-"influence" rhetoric. Frederick Hoxie, president of ASE during 1997, revisited this ground in his presidential address to the organization's annual convention, titled "Ethnohistory for a Tribal World," condemning what he calls "contributionist" history.

Hoxie is a historian with a penchant for more than simply writing history. He is also a gatekeeper, an arbiter of ethnohistorical correctness, one who takes as his role the instruction of other historians what (to borrow Noam Chomsky's phrase) is inside and outside of the realm of permissible debate. Hoxie is not content to tell his own story and let others tell theirs. He is interested in establishing a party line by which some stories are told and other lines of inquiry shut down. Certain "scholarly paths," he tells us, "are no longer helpful" (Hoxie, 600). "...A path that does not need expansion is represented by books from the 'contributions' school..." which Hoxie says are authored by "romantic polemicists" (Hoxie, 602). The fact that Hoxie dismisses the whole idea of Iroquois influence on democracy without engaging the historical facts does not seem, to him, to qualify what he writes as a "polemic." He saves that word, with all its negative connotations, for those whose "angle on the fire" he dislikes -- Jack Weatherford and his (as Hoxie puts it, tossing in a personal insult) "less able colleagues," including, by name, the compiler of this bibliography. (Hoxie, 603, 605)

To Hoxie, the "polemical writings" of the "contributionist" approach are "simplistic," wearing "dull academic uniforms," involving "abuses and distortions," to be "set aside" (Hoxie, 606-607). Writers of such histories are said, by Hoxie, to resemble "cabaret pianists who talk about baseball while playing their repertoire of standards...engag[ing]...ultimately [in] secondary and superficial conversations with ethnohistorical materials" (Hoxie, 605-606). Dazzled by Hoxie's imagery and bemused by one of the weirdest pieces of *ad hominem* rhetoric in his personal memory, this reader is left to assume, perhaps, that Professor Hoxie plays *his* piano in a renowned symphony, or at least uptown at the Ritz.

Professor Hoxie is not engaging in historical analysis, since his narrative does not engage a single historical fact in the "influence" debate. Rather, he is acting as a gatekeeper who reserves privileges for himself that plain-vanilla academic grunts do not enjoy, and, in so doing not only unfairly (and personally) demeans his opponents with searing polemics of his own, but seeks to shut them out of ethnohistorically correct debate, as he "officially" defines it. In this "conversation," Hoxie, by virtue of his exalted position, does all the talking.

Regarding Hoxie and other "Iroquois experts," Mohawk writer and activist Doug George-Kanentiio comments that "Some professionals grudgingly acknowledge that the Haudenosaunee (Iroquois) were the most influential indigenous people in North America, yet they dig in their heels at the thought that the Iroquois might have sparked the democratic ideals of the founders of the infant United States." (George)

William Starna, writing with George Hamell, condemned the idea vehemently in *New York History*. Usually, when scholars' ideas are attacked with such unabashed vigor, journal editors offer rebuttal space, as before, with us, in *Ethnohistory* and the *William and Mary*

*Quarterly.* In this case, Starna and Hamell's piece found its way to us through a chain of friends nearly a year after its publication date, too late for an effective reply.

Starna and Hamell must have spent many hours ransacking footnotes in *Exemplar of Liberty* and other works. They find a handful of factual errors which they admit are minor. The problem here is that Starna and Hamell are so engaged in debunking details that they do not address any of the ideas that were communicated between the Iroquois and colonial Americans. Instead they debate, with excruciating attention to detail, whether Canassatego had brawny arms, and whether he was known for being unsociably direct after he had had a few drinks. As an elicitation of historical truth, this argument rings rather hollow. The piece is really ideologically driven character assassination masquerading as historical criticism. Starna and Hammel find errors like Senator Joseph McCarthy used to locate communists, blowing a few minor errors into an asserted conspiracy to perpetrate what they regard as a gigantic intellectual fraud. Their line of reasoning has been borrowed from another steadfast critic of the idea, Elisabeth Tooker.

In their rush to condemn, Starna and Hamell fail to extend their ambit beyond the debate over Iroquois influences on the Albany Plan, beginning with the words of Canassatego at the Lancaster Treaty Council of 1744. They ignore most of our case, which takes the "influence" idea from the early seventeenth century to the end of the nineteenth. They also restrict their inquiry to New York sources, forgetting, perhaps, that representatives from other colonies (notably Pennsylvania) sent representatives to the important events of the time, who left records in their respective archives. Starna and Hamell all but accuse us of fabricating evidence that is available to anyone in the archives of Pennsylvania, Massachusetts, and Virginia.

Those who are ready for some *real* academic mudwrestling may wish to consult Alvin J. Schmidt's *Menace of Multiculturalism.* As his title indicates, Schmidt, a professor of sociology at Illinois College, Jacksonville, is a take-no-prisoners opponent of multiculturalism. At the beginning of a chapter titled "The Facts Be Damned," Schmidt lists a number of "facts" that he says multiculturalists have "invented." One of these is that "the Constitution of the United States was shaped by the Iroquois Indians." (Schmidt, 43-44) He also denies the idea that Crispus Attucks, the first casualty of the Boston Massacre, was black (Attucks' father was black. His mother was Native American). Since he has never heard of any of the many books and articles documenting it, Schmidt says that the "influence" idea is "undocumented." Schmidt would rather history stress the cruel and violent aspects of Native American cultures, which he says squishy-soft multiculturalists downplay. Schmidt is barely getting warmed up. Later in the book, he argues that American Indian cultures were environmentally destructive and that women in native societies lived "in virtual slavery." Returning to the Iroquois influence issue, Schmidt calls it a "fabrication," as well as "historical fiction." (Schmidt, 53-54)

As the contemporary debate has raged, one unexpected result of my most recent research has been a large number of older mentions of the "influence" idea. Many of these references surfaced in the context of reading with other objectives (most of it while writing a number of reference books for Greenwood Press). Strung together, these references reveal an impressive lineage from Lewis Henry Morgan through Frederich Engels, Elizabeth Cady Stanton, and Matilda Joslyn Gage. The idea popped up in *New York Times* editorials during 1873 and 1893, and in a general survey of American Indian societies first published in 1855.

In a survey of Native American cultures in the Western Hemisphere, first published in 1855, Charles de Wolf Brownell wrote that "The nature of the [Iroquois] league was decidedly democratic; arbitrary power was lodged in the hands of no ruler....A singular unanimity was generally observed in their councils" (Brownell, 287). Brownell then added, on the same page: "We are told that for a long period before the [American] revolution, the Iroquois chiefs and orators held up their own confederation as an example for the imitation of the English colonies." By whom Brownell was told this, he does not say. It is possible that Brownell read the assertion in one of the early editions of Lewis Henry Morgan's *League of the Haudenosaunee, or Iroquois* (1851). Nearly a century after the pivotal events that formed the United States, Morgan characterized the Iroquois League as a federal model very much like the new nation: "The nations [of the Iroquois League] sustained nearly the same relation to the league that the American states bear to the Union. In the former, several oligarchies are combined within one, in the same manner as [in] the latter, several republics are embraced in one republic." (Morgan, 3)

Sometimes, new information creates historical riddles. For example, someone, very likely an Iroquois (a Seneca in one account, a Cayuga in two), expressed an opinion in 1808 (one account) or 1847 (two accounts) saying that the United States founding generation stood at the Longhouse door, and counted itself lucky to get the sweepings. Was it an unidentified Cayuga chief in 1808 (Armstrong, 42), Dr. Peter Wilson, a Cayuga, in 1847 (McLuhan, 100 ), or Ely S. Parker, a Seneca who served as secretary to General U.S. Grant, in 1847? (Parker, 1847). The record yields three possible authors of what is essentially the same sentence. The reference is said to have appeared in a paper, "Territorial Limits, Geographical Names and Trails of the Iroquois," which was read by Dr. Peter Wilson, a Cayuga, at a meeting of the New York Historical Society during 1847. Wilson said: "Have we, the first holders of this prosperous region, no longer a share in your history.

Glad were your fathers to sit upon the threshold of the Long House, rich did they hold themselves in getting the mere sweepings from its door." McLuhan's source for this quotation is Lewis H. Morgan, *League of the Hodenosaunee, or Iroquois* (1851), in a 1904 edition published by Dodd-Mead (Book 3, pp. 104-105), a fourth possible source.

At the turn of the century, the noted ethnographer of the Iroquois William N. Beauchamp took up the subject. While discussing the federal structure of the Iroquois Confederacy, Beauchamp writes that "Local affairs were left to national councils, as in our general and state governments." Beauchamp also writes that "...the chiefs do not seem to have worn any distinctive badge....This is one of the curious resemblances in our national political system and that of the Iroquois. " (Beauchamp, 342, 437)

Early in the twentieth century, the Seneca Arthur Parker annotated his version of the Great Law of Peace with this statement: "Here, then, we find the right of popular nomination, the right of recall and of woman suffrage flourishing in the old America of the Red Man...centuries before it became the clamor of the new America of the white invader. Who now shall call the Indians and the Iroquois savages?" (Parker, 1968, 11)

In a survey of American Indians published by the Smithsonian in 1929 (republished in 1934), Rose Palmer undertakes a detailed description of the Iroquois League, including its founding story and political organization. As part of this description, she writes: "It was an extraordinary genius for social organization, which culminated in a confederation that endured through two centuries and in some respects served as a model for the union of the Colonies" (Palmer, 81). I was surprised to find a school curriculum that took up the idea of Iroquois contributions to democracy, dated 1972, in Oakland, California. (Beals, 1972)

I continue to be amazed at the scope of the debate, and the many audiences it has reached. Notable skirmishes in the debate have taken place in unlikely venues, such as Canada's *Financial Post* (Frum, 1998; Hipwell, 1998). In Illinois, mention that the "influence" idea played a role in the state assessment test for public-school students was enough to compel introduction of a bill to change the test (O'Connor, 1998). The idea also has been presented to a Japanese audience. (Hoshikawa, 1997), and has been taken up in French and English newspapers.

The "influence" idea has even made waves in the U.S. Navy. During the fall of 1995, Washington *Times* Columnist John McCaslin ridiculed Chief of Naval Operations Admiral Jeremy Boorda for sending a directive to "all commands on land and sea" honoring Native American contributions to democracy in observance of Native American Heritage Month in November. "And you thought the great genius of our

form of government was bequeathed by that race of kings across yonder
ocean -- the Magna Carta, the commonlaw, and all that? But it wasn't,
according to eminent historian and political scientist Jeremy Boorda,
who moonlights as chief of naval operations." Adm. Boorda had
encouraged all commands to "support programs and exhibits, publish
items of interest in command bulletins, and promote maximum
participation by military and civilian personnel." McCaslin quotes an
unnamed "senior veteran" as calling this the silly season of politically
correct admirals. The veteran is quoted as saying "I don't know
whether to laugh or cry." (McCaslin, A-5)

Mary Lefkowitz, a professor of Classics at Wellesley College,
left me with another intriguing e-mail tidbit that I was not
able to confirm with a published source until later: that the
noted feminist Gloria Steinem had talked about the Iroquois role in the
origins of democracy in a commencement speech at Wellesley. Professor
Lefkowitz said she had heard the speech. I never was able to find a
copy of that speech, but I did learn, through Sally Roesch Wagner,
that Steinem was preparing to cite some of Wagner's research on
Iroquois foundations of nineteenth-century feminism in an historical
anthology. (Steinem) This survey work includes two chapters on the
origins of feminism, one of which includes excerpts from Sally Roesch
Wagner's work describing how the thoughts of Matilda Joslyn Gage and
Elizabeth Cady Stanton were shaped by their association with
Iroquois women in the mid and late nineteenth century.
    As I was taking this volume to press, I found an interview with
Steinem in the San Francisco *Chronicle* about her new book. The
interviewer, Patricia Holt, writes that Steinem's most notable
discovery in writing this book, "was the realization that the Iroquois
Confederacy of six major northeastern tribes 'inspired the structure of
the U.S. Constitution, a fact only recently acknowledged in legal
history,' its matrilineal society inspired the suffragist movement."
Holt's account continues: "'The Iroquois guaranteed the social and
political power of women to such an extent," says Steinem, "'That
suffragists like Elizabeth Cady Stanton and Susan B. Anthony, who
talked and listened to women from the nearby tribes, were able to
imagine a life of equality they had never known.'" (Holt, 2)
    Steinem's speech at Wellesley provided the gist for the
beginning of Lefkowitz's *Wall Street Journal* review of *The Menace of
Multiculturalism*:

> Does the U.S. Constitution owe more to the 18th-century
> Iroquois than it does to the ancient Greeks? No, but many
> younger people may answer yes, because it is what they have
> learned in school. The history that children learn is not
> necessarily a record of what actually happened in the past;

rather, it is often an account of what parents and teachers believe they ought to know. (Lefkowitz, A-16)

Later in her review, Lefkowitz wrote that "However impressive the governmental organization of the Iroquois nation, the inspiration behind the Constitution may once again be credited to the European Enlightenment, and the ancient Greeks" (Lefkowitz, A-16). Lefkowitz, the author of *Not Out of Africa,* a widely quoted critique of Afrocentric education, is much more practiced at protecting the Greeks from purported African influences than shielding the United States' founders from Iroquois ones. Replying to Lefkowitz in the *Wall Street Journal's* letters column April 10, 1997, I said that giving credit to the Iroquois does not demean classical Greek or English precedents for United States basic law, but "simply add[s] an Iroquois role to the picture." I concluded: "We can have our Greeks, and our Iroquois, too." (Johansen, A-15)

A week after his letter was published, I found a message in my e-mail inbox from Professor Lefkowitz, who acknowledged my main point: that we can study the Iroquois system and its impact on subsequent history without packing up the Greek and the Magna Carta and sending them, along with the rest of Europe's classical history, back across the ocean. She also thanked me for sources on the debate, and said that she had modified *Not Out of Africa* in paperback to take account of criticism. "I never doubted that the Iroquois and other Native Americans gave ideas to the European settlers," she wrote. "All I was questioning was the proportion."

During these exchanges, we seemed to be seeking a middle ground where a consensus of our history may settle, with regard to Native American influences, once the debates have been had and the feathers have flown, at the beginning of a new millennium on the Christian calendar. The middle ground that we seemed to be seeking also has been explored tentatively by Peter D. Salins in his book *Assimilation, American Style* (1997).

As Americans were differentiating themselves from their nominal or actual English ancestors in the realm of ideas, attitudes, and values, whatever remained of English cultural influences was also being progressively diluted by their contact with an ever-expanding array of non-English peoples. First, the European settlers were changed by contact with the real "native" Americans...who introduced them to new foods, new arts and crafts, new modes of shelter, new strategies for survival in the wilderness, and perhaps even some important civic principles. (Salins, 90)

Vine Deloria, Jr.'s critique of the debate traces its intensity in our time more to academic power politics than to a search for historical veracity. "This fight over the Six Nations' influence has been a bitter one, and if it had been submitted to a jury for fair deliberation the anthropological profession would now be paying reparations to the Six Nations, for the evidence and the argument weigh heavily in favor of the Iroquois and their supporters." (Biolsi, 215)

In *The Journal of the West,* Deloria responded to concerns expressed by Francis Paul Prucha in the January, 1995 issue of the same publication that

> The gap is widening, I fear, between solid historical accounts and the pseudohistorical or mythical accounts adopted and proclaimed by many Indians and their white advocates....A good example, which h as been around from [sic] some years, is the effort to make the Iroquois Confederacy the [sic] model for the United States Constitution and American democratic government. Books and articles advancing these claims have appeared, and they have been refuted by knowledgeable scholars...but the idea continues to get support....The differences between the Iroquois League and the Constitution are numerous and significant, but even granting similarities, to conclude that one was the model for the other is a simple *post hoc ergo propter hoc* fallacy. (Prucha, 3-4)

Instead, wrote Deloria, "The truth is that the discipline of historical writing is beginning to move from its centuries-long simplistic doctrinal interpretation of history as a *good white man-bad Indian* scenario." Deloria believes that "The real issue underlying Prucha's complaint is based on authority and status. His examples of revisionist, and presumably inaccurate, history and his descriptive language illustrate what I would call the pitiful complaint and anguish of the old orthodoxy" (Deloria, 3-4). Deloria then outlines the idea that the Iroquois helped shape democratic thought, and says that such ideas "were not refuted" by Prucha, "They were simply attacked." Deloria continues: "The point that the old school apparently misses is that one of the critical issues faced by the constitutional generation was the distribution of sovereign political powers between the new federal government and the colonies." The Six Nations had long since resolved this problem, he believes. "[I]t seems absurd to continue to maintain that the founding fathers choose the course they did out of sheer genius." Deloria scoffs, as well, as the belief that "Andrew Jackson was the best friend Indians ever had," a reference to earlier writings by Prucha. He concludes: "Scholars should not worry that pristine historical study is undermined by new ideas or efforts to correct ancient wrongs. *That is the nature of continuing scholarship.*" (Deloria, 3-4, emphasis in original)

**FURTHER READING:**

Armstrong, Virginia Irving. *I Have Spoken: American History Through the Voices of the Indians.* Chicago: Swallow Press, 1971.

Beals, Katie and John J. Carusone. *Native Americans: The Constitution of the Iroquois League.* Oakland, Calif.: United School District, 1972.

Beauchamp, William M. *Civil, Religious, and Mourning Councils and Ceremonies of Adoption of the New York Indians.* New York State Museum Bulletin No. 113. Albany, N.Y.: New York State Education Department, June, 1907.

Biolsi, Thomas and Larry J. Zimmerman, eds. *Indians and Anthropologists: Vine Deloria, Jr., and the Critique of Anthropology.* Tucson: University of Arizona Press, 1997.

Bork, Robert H. *Slouching Toward Gomorrah: Modern Liberalism and American Decline.* San Francisco: ReganBooks/HarperCollins, 1996.

Brownell, Charles de Wolf. *The Indian Races of America: A General View.* Boston: Dayton and Wentworth, 1855.

Deloria, Vine, Jr. "The Western Forum: The Struggle for Authority." *Journal of the West* 34:3 (July, 1995), pp. 3-4.

Foreman, Jonathan. "Film I: Big Bad Brits (and Other Myths)." *National Review*, April 20, 1998.

Frum, David. "Champions of Native Rights Spin Fabrications About the Past: Let's Set the Record Straight on Native History." *The Financial Post* (Ottawa), February 7, 1998, p. 20.

George, Doug (Kanentiio). "The Founding Date for the Haudenosaunee Confederacy." Syracuse *Herald-American*, Editorial pages, May 17, 1998.

Hipwell, Bill. "Apology Should Have Been a Thank You." *The Financial Post* (Ottawa) February 3, 1998, p. 18.

Holt, Patricia. "Steinem Edits a History of U.S. Women." San Francisco *Chronicle*, April 19, 1998, p. 2 "Sunday Review."

Hoshikawa, Jun. *Pacific Rim Innernet Journeys: Wisdom of the Mongoloid Indigenous Peoples.* Tokyo: NTT Publishing, 1997.

Hoxie, Frederick. "Ethnohistory in a Tribal World." *Ethnohistory* 44:4(Fall, 1997), pp. 595-616.

Johansen, Bruce E. "The Iroquois: Present at the Birth." *Wall Street Journal* [Letter to the editor], April 10, 1997, p. A-15.

Lefkowitz, Mary. "Out of Many, More Than One." *Wall Street Journal,* March 24, 1997, p. A-16.

McCaslin, John. "Inside the Beltway: The Great Pumpkin Speaks." Washington *Times,* October 26, 1995, p. A-5.

McLuhan, T.C. *Touch the Earth: A Self-Portrait of Indian Existence.* New York: Outerbridge and Lazard, 1971.

Moquin, Wayne. *Great Documents in American Indian History.* New York: Praeger Publishers, 1973.

Morgan, Lewis Henry. *League of the Haudenosaunee, or Iroquois.* [1851] New York: Dodd, Mead & Co., 1922.

O'Connor, John. "Bill That Would Remove 'Subjective' Questions from ISAP Advances." Copley News Service, March 11, 1998. [in LEXIS]

Palmer, Rose. *The North American Indians: An Account of the American Indians North of Mexico, Compiled from the Original Sources.* Volume Four of the Smithsonian Scientific Series. [1929] Washington, D.C.: The Smithsonian Institution, 1934.

Parker, Arthur C. "The Constitution of the Five Nations," in William N. Fenton, ed., *Parker on the Iroquois.* Syracuse, N.Y.: Syracuse University Press, 1968.

Parker, Ely S. "Address to the New York State Historical Society, May 27, 1847," in Ely S. Parker Papers, Reel 1, American Philosophical Society.

Prucha, Francis Paul. "Western Forum: The Challenge of Indian History." *The Journal of the West* 34:1(January, 1995), pp. 3-4.

Salins, Peter D. *Assimilation, American Style.* San Francisco: New Republic/HarperCollins, 1997.

Schlafly, Phyllis. "National Standards Mean National Control." Copley News Service, September 9, 1997 [in LEXIS].

Schmidt, Alvin J. *The Menace of Multiculturalism.* Westport, Conn.: Praeger, 1997.

Snow, Dean R. *The Iroquois.* Oxford, U.K.: Blackwell, 1994.

Starna, William A. and George R. Hamell. "History and the Burden of Proof: The Case of the Iroquois Influence on the U.S. Constitution." *New York History,* October, 1996, 427-452.

Steinem, Gloria, Wilma Mankiller, Marysa Navarro, Barbara Smith, and Wendy Mink, eds. *Reader's Guide to U.S. Women's History.* Boston: Houghton-Mifflin, 1998.

# Acknowledgments

Many thanks to John Kahionhes Fadden, Donald A. Grinde, Jr., Jose Barreiro, Shelly Price-Jones, Sally Roesch-Wagner, Christine Kasel, Steve Witala, Jeremy Lipschultz, Scott Calbeck, Diane Carpenter-Crews, Barbara Mann, Doug George/Kanentiio, Dale Stover, Jerry Stubben, and Bruce A. Burton for providing titles from their files. Renewed gratitude is also due the incredible bibliographic sleuths of the University of Nebraska at Omaha Interlibrary Loan Office.

# Bibliographic Entries

## 1998

### Books, Scholarly, and Specialty Publications

**1998.001.** _____. [Review, Johansen, *Encyclopedia of Native American Legal Tradition*] *Booklist*, May 1, 1998, p. 1542.

> *Booklist's* unsigned review says that "This encyclopedia is highly recommended for any examination or investigation of constitutional or judicial law in the U.S. It will find use in a public, high-school, or academic library. It will round out many studies and give a fresh perspective to the 'founding' of this democracy."

**1998.002.** Castile, George Pierre. *To Show Heart: Native American Self-Determination and Federal Indian Policy*, 1960-1975. Tucson: University of Arizona Press, 1998.

> On page 14, Castile notes that President John F. Kennedy contributed a preface to Alvin Josephy's *American Heritage Book of Indians* (1961) that said: "[T]he League of the Iroquois inspired Benjamin Franklin to copy it in the planning of the federation of states." Castile says that the Preface was written by an unknown author in the Interior Department who was being advised by Pierre Salinger, JFK's press secretary. Castile says: "This is a story, like President Millard Fillmore's installation of the first White House bathtub, that has gained authority by repetition." He cites an article by Johansen in the *American Indian Culture & Research Journal* (1990) and Elisabeth Tooker's 1988 article in *Ethnohistory*.

**1998.003.** Deloria, Philip J. *Playing Indian*. New Haven: Yale University Press, 1998.

On page 79, Deloria quotes Lewis Henry Morgan: "The Indian is also a Republican and this is more truly a fact than may at first appear." In an extended footnote ["Address by Schenandoah," August 9, 1843. See also: Bieder, "Grand Order of the Iroquois," 358(pp. 219-220)], Deloria writes that "Ironically, more than a century later, scholars have been debating exactly this point-- the depth of influence the form and procedures of the Iroquois league might have had on founding Americans' ideas about constitutional government." *Forgotten Founders, Exemplar of Liberty*, and the Johansen-Tooker exchange in *Ethnohistory* are referenced. Deloria's work is a study of ways in which images of Indians have shaped non-Indian culture in the United States; on pp. 28-29, for example, he writes that Indian images were the most popular patriotic symbols during the Revolutionary War: "Between 1765 and 1783, the Colonies appeared as an Indian in no fewer than sixty-five political prints -- almost four times as frequently as the other main symbols of America, the snake and the child."

**1998.004.** Eberhart, George M. [Review, Johansen, *Encyclopedia of Native American Legal Tradition*] *College and Research Libraries News*, June, 1998, p. 454.

In his regular column, "New Publications," Eberhart remarks that "few visitors to the site of the first English colony at Jamestown are aware that representative government in America was practiced by Native Americans centuries before European contact and that the Iroquois Confederacy was one of John Adams' models for his vision of the U.S. Constitution. Eberhart calls this book "an essential work for legal and Native American collections."

**1998.005.** Fenton, William N. *The Great Law and the Longhouse: A Political History of the Iroquois Confederacy*. Norman: University of Oklahoma Press, 1998.

On page 5, Fenton maintains that no one outside the Iroquois League understood its operations before Lewis Henry Morgan in 1851: "Neither Cadwallader Colden...Sir William Johnson...nor the framers of the United States Constitution give evidence that they knew or understood it [the Iroquois League] or that Iroquois statesmen had communicated it to them. That something so fundamental to Iroquois political philosophy escaped the notice of early writers on Iroquois manners is a problem in intellectual history." After dismissing Colden's knowledge on page 5, Fenton (whose index contains 46 references to Colden) pays him this backhanded compliment on page 357: "Until Cadwallader Colden (1727), English sources show a singular lack of insight into the nature of Iroquois government." On page 403, Fenton mentions Franklin's "sustained fascination with the Iroquois Confederacy," but on page 432, after quoting Canassatego's advice that the colonies should unite at the 1744 Lancaster Treaty, he finds this idea of interest only "as a source of amusement among the English intelligentsia." To Fenton, Canassatego's advice "suggested the germ of confederation without the structure for accomplishing it." Fenton, on page 471, also cites Franklin's advice to his printing partner James Parker (in 1751) that the colonies combine in a union similar to that of the Iroquois, commenting that the quote "has of late inspired proponents of the idea that the writers of the United States Constitution derived its structure and separation of powers from the Iroquois Confederacy, a doctrine for which supporting historical evidence has escaped responsible scholars....Like much of what is advanced today as politically correct, this spurious doctrine represents invented tradition." At this point, Fenton cites Tooker and Johansen's debate over the idea in *Ethnohistory* (1988, 1990). Fenton repeats his assertion on page 475: "Nowhere in the document [the Albany Plan], or in the negotiations leading up to it, does one find evidence that the Iroquois projected a model of their league or confederacy or that the commissioners understood its structure and operation." The influence case, to Fenton, is "current dogma." On page 592, however, Fenton reviews the treaty council at German Flats, New York (1775), at which colonial commissioners recalled Canassatego's advice in 1744. Without an apparent sense of contradiction, Fenton finds this to be "the first solid evidence of the impact of the Iroquois Confederacy as a model for the united colonies."

**1998.006.** Grinde, Donald A., Jr., "Thomas Jefferson's Dualistic Approach to American Indians" in Evelyn Sinclair and James Gilcreast, eds. *Thomas Jefferson and the Education of the Citizen.* Washington, D.C.: Library of Congress/Government Printing Office, 1998.

This volume was published in observance of the 250th anniversary of Jefferson's birth. Grinde describes ways in which Jefferson's thinking was shaped by his associations with Native American peoples and nations. Historians Gordon

Wood, Merrill Peterson, Holly Brewer, Richard Matthews, and others also contributed to this volume.

**1998.007.** Johansen, Bruce E., ed. *The Encyclopedia of Native American Legal Tradition.* Westport, Conn.: Greenwood Press, 1998.

This book contains detailed treatments of Iroquois and other Native American polities, with tracing of influence on the United States' political development. This link is also noted in entries on Canassatego and Hendrick.

**1998.008.** Johansen, Bruce E. "Declaration of Independence," in David Bradley and Shelly Fisher Fishkin, eds. *The Encyclopedia of Civil Rights in America.* New York: M.E. Sharpe, 1998, 3 vols.

Under "Declaration of Independence" (I:296-298), Johansen discusses Iroquois contributions to "life, liberty, and the pursuit of happiness," citing the writings of Thomas Jefferson, in the context of European thought during the Enlightenment.

**1998.009.** Kinneavy, James L. and John E. Warriner. *Elements of Writing, Complete Course.* Austin, Tex.: Holt, Rinehart and Winston, 1998.

On page 457, as part of a writing exercise, this high-school English textbook describes Canassatego's advice to the colonists to unite on an Iroquois model in 1744, Benjamin Franklin's use of the Iroquois model, and his 1754 Albany Plan. The exercise, which appears with artwork by Mohawk John Kahionhes Fadden, concludes: "Benjamin Franklin is a clear link between the Iroquois League and the founding of our nation. He knew and admired the League's government and suggested it as a model for the colonies. He very likely brought these ideas to the Constitutional Convention." The book cites and quotes from *Forgotten Founders* (1982, 1987).

**1998.010.** Laduke, Winona. "Indigenous Women," in Shapiro, Eddie and Debbie, eds. *Voices from the Heart: A Compassionate Call for Responsibility.* New York: Putnam, 1998.

Laduke, on pp. 26-27, writes that "it has been said that the U. S. form of democracy was founded on the concepts of the Iroquois Confederacy....But the founding fathers missed a very essential point. In the Iroquois six-nation confederacy, the clan mothers had the right to appoint and depose chiefs....The founding fathers did not even give women the right to vote." Part of the conquest of Europe over America was the conquest of patriarchy over matriarchy, Laduke says.

**1998.011.** Levine, Ellen. *If You Lived With the Iroquois...* New York: Scholastic Publishers, 1998.

This children's book observes that "A growing number of historians believe" that the Iroquois Great Law of Peace "had a lasting effect on the American government." Levine says that Benjamin Franklin "greatly admired the Iroquois form of government," and took from it attributes of federalism, balance of power and checks and balances, a belief that governors are servants of the people rather than their masters.

**1998.012.** Lobo, Susan and Steven Talbot, eds. *Native American Voices: A Reader.* New York: Longman Publishers, 1998.

This college-level reader contains essays by various authors on a number of subjects related to Native American history and cultures. Among them is "Perceptions of America's Democracies," by Grinde and Johansen, from *Exemplar of Liberty* (1991), pp. 72-82. The influence issue also is mentioned on pages 57 and 116; *Exemplar of Liberty* (1991), *Forgotten Founders* (1982) and Donald Grinde's *The Iroquois and the Founding of the American Nation* (1977) are referenced.

**1998.013.** Schlesinger, Arthur M., Jr. *The Disuniting of America: Reflections on a Multicutural Society.* Revised and enlarged edition. New York: W. W. Norton, 1998.

This edition is largely a replating of the 1992 book, with added sources and a denunciation of "monoculturalists" on the right wing, to balance Schlesinger's condemnation of "multiculuralists" on the left. Schlesinger displays no knowledge of what became of the New York Curriculum of Inclusion (including its Native American component *Haudenosaunee: Past, Present, Future*) during the six years since this book's initial publication. The Haudenosaunee curriculum was not adopted by New York public schools. Instead, the state education department ceded ownership of it to the Haudenosaunee Grand Council. Schlesinger still shows no awareness of the considerable debate over assertions that the

Iroquois helped shape the character of democracy. He chooses to remain ignorant of the published record as well, preferring buzzwords to describe the idea, such as "feel-good" history, which he believes to be a product of a "cult of multiculturalism," a brush with which he also amply paints "afrocentric" curricula.

**1998.014.** Skidmore, Max. *Legacy to the World: A Study of America's Political Ideas.* New York: Peter Lang Publishing, 1998.

Skidmore's examination of how American political ideas have affected world political systems includes extensive treatment of Iroquois political institutions and the ways in which the founders of the United States used them, citing from various works by Grinde and Johansen, especially *Exemplar of Liberty*, on ms. pp. 60-65. After examining the debate over the issue, Skidmore writes (ms. p. 65) that their argument "seems to be a reasoned, and reasonable, conclusion."

**1998.015.** Steinem, Gloria, Wilma Mankiller, Marysa Navarro, Barbara Smith, and Wendy Mink, eds. *Reader's Guide to U.S. Women's History.* Boston: Houghton-Mifflin, 1998.

This survey work includes two chapters on the origins of feminism, one of which includes excerpts from Sally Roesch Wagner's work describing how the thoughts of Matilda Joslyn Gage and Elizabeth Cady Stanton were shaped by their association with Iroquois women in the mid and late nineteenth century.

**1998.016.** Weatherford, Jack. [Review, Calloway, *New Worlds for All*] *William and Mary Quarterly* Third Ser., Vol. 55:1(January, 1998), pp. 143-144.

Weatherford writes that Calloway does a good job of uniting "the story of native peoples with that of the many groups, nations and races that poured into North America after 1492" (p. 143). Within this context, "Calloway picks his way carefully across a wide swath of territory and always offers reasoned interpretations....For example, he gives a conservative overview of the issues related to Indian influence on the development of American democracy. In this regard, he helps to tone down some unnecessarily ideological rhetoric on this topic and returns the discussion to a more moderate and reasoned, although incomplete, discourse."

## *Newspapers and Trade Magazines*

**1998.017.** _____. "On Home Video." San Diego *Union-Tribune*, September 12, 1998, p. E-2.

> This piece reviews three new episodes of the children's video, "Adventures of Elmer and Friends." Elmer is a talking tree who makes regular journeys into the past, taking a troupe of children, with the help of items provided by a curio-shop owner. In one of the three videos, "Freedom Rocks," the whole gang travels back in time to meet an Iroquois woman who is played by renowned Oneida folk-singer Joanne Shenandoah. The woman teaches the children Iroquois games, and "also talks about human rights, reiterating the words of the United States Constitution, and how they apply to all people."

**1998.018.** _____. "Economic Crises, War on Terrorism, Crippled Presidency -- A Conversation with Twentysomethings on the New World Disorder." Pacific News Service, September 18, 1998.

> This commentary is a collection of extended interviews with people in their 20s about the problems facing the United States at a national level. One of them, "Jackie," comments: "When I look at the Clinton presidency, I really think about how this country was founded on ideas of government that came from native people. The United States Constitution and form of government is based on the Iroquois Confederacy -- a lot of the founding fathers spoke Iroquois. The big difference is that in the Iroquois Confederacy only women voted -- the grandmothers chose who was going to lead based on a long observation of the person, on an idea of their entire character."

**1998.019.** Abello, Thomas. "Six Nations Indian Museum Keeps a Tradition Alive." *Adirondack Daily Enterprise* [Saranac Lake, N.Y.], August 1, 1998, p. B-1.

> This feature story on the Fadden family's Six Nations Indian Museum (Onchiota, New York) says that it "has become a true Adirondack treasure." In the article, John Kahionhes Fadden is quoted as saying "Europeans were introduced to three-quarters of the food they eat and the concepts of democracy

when they came here."

**1998.020.** Barlow, James Herbert. "Sow Seeds of Belonging to Reap Peace." Rochester [New York] *Democrat and Chronicle*, June 24, 1998.

> In an editorial-page column, Barlow describes the activities of Mohawk culture bearer Jake Swamp and the Tree of Peace Society, noting that the eagle and bundle of arrows (part of the U.S. Seal) on the dollar bill originally were Iroquois symbols. "In 1987," writes Barlow, "the U.S. Senate passed a resolution honoring the fact that the Iroquois Confederacy served Franklin, Madison, Jefferson, and Washington as a model for the U.S. Constitution."

**1998.021.** Cardwell, Lynda, Michelle Suarez, and Anna Manring. "Education: Smart Resources For Students and Parents; Where Homework and the Internet Meet; Launchpoint: Native Americans." Los Angeles *Times*, August 31, 1998, p. B-2.

> This is a cooperative educational effort by the Los Angeles *Times* and the Education Department of the University of California--Irving which combines columns in the newspaper (on a weekly basis) with various Internet websites. The column for August 31 began: "The Iroquois Nation's democratic government has been operating successfully for hundreds of years and greatly influenced the drafting of the U.S. Constitution."
> See also: http://www.latimes.com/launchpoint/

**1998.022.** Cross, Dan. "Indian Museum A Family Business." *The Eastern Door* [Kahnawake Mohawk Territory]. August 28, 1998, p. 11.

> This a feature on the Fadden family's Six Nations Indian Museum, in which John Kahionhes Fadden observes, "I try to continue as my father (Ray, now 88 years of age) did, speaking of the traditional government and how advanced it was and still is. As a matter of fact, the U.S. Constitution was influenced by our own Constitution. The difference is that they referred to Mother Earth in monetary terms."

**1998.023.** Enman, Charles. "Stars in a Native Sky." Ottawa *Citizen*, July 1, 1998, p. A-6.

The lives of ten leading Native Americans are briefly outlined in this piece, including Hiawatha, "the force behind the creation of the Iroquois League of Five Nations, a democratic experiment created around 1450 that may have partly inspired the democratic visions of early American philosophers." Enman quotes from Cadwallader Colden on the nature of the league, and says that Franklin's Albany Plan of Union (1754) "drew direct inspiration from Hiawatha's League."

**1998.024.** Foreman, Jonathan. "Film I: Big Bad Brits (and Other Myths)." *National Review*, April 20, 1998.

Foreman is bemoaning his belief that "Baby Boomers" have infected Hollywood movies with liberal values based on their "generational experience" in the 1960s. Collectively, Foreman argues, these "Boomers" are shaping the media with their "delusions." He moans, by way of letting his conservative audience know just how stupid the "Boomers" can be, that "We live in a society where some students are taught that the United States Constitution was inspired by the Iroquois, that the Greeks stole science from Africans, and that the Aztecs were sweeties who didn't really eat people like popcorn." In this way, Foreman argues that "Boomers" like to have their prejudices confirmed.

**1998.025.** Frum, David. "Champions of Native Rights Spin Fabrications About the Past: Let's Set the Record Straight on Native History." *The Financial Post* (Ottawa), February 7, 1998, p. 20.

David Frum, columnist for the *Financial Post* of Ottawa, having endured several contrary letters to the editor after his first attempt to assert that Europeans did Native Americans a favor by colonizing the Americas, comes back for more, in which he asserts that the idea that the Iroquois have anything to do with democracy is "pure invention." In his conservative column ("What's Right"), Frum reacts to Bill Hipwell's letter (below), among others, as he calls the idea that American Indians had anything to do with the development of democracy "an invention," and part of "a pseudo-history of North America designed to enhance the prestige of native culture...[which] is now seeping from the small ideological subgroups that created it into the larger society." When the advocates of the U.S. Constitution sought precedents, writes Frum, "they did what any educated eighteenth-century gentlemen would have done -- they rummaged through the history of Greece and Rome." Frum never entertains the idea that European and Native American precedents could have been combined by the Founders. He maintains that the ideas in the Constitution came solely from Aristotle, through English common law. This column also was printed in the Toronto *Sun* on the same date.

**1998.026.** Gammage, Jeff. "Thousands Gather to Mark Women's Rights Movement." New Orleans *Times-Picayune*, July 19, 1998, p. A-2.

This lengthy account of the Seneca Falls' conference's 150th anniversary observes that "Cashiers at Sonnenberg Gardens in nearby Canandaigua were giving Susan B. Anthony dollars as change. Lecturers lauded the role of Iroquois Indians in the women's struggle." A longer account of the same article appeared in the Houston *Chronicle*, July 17, 1998, p. A-4. Gammage is a reporter for the Philadelphia *Inquirer*.

**1998.027.** George, Doug (Kanentiio). "The Founding Date for the Haudenosaunee Confederacy." Syracuse *Herald-American*, Editorial pages, May 17, 1998.

In the context of information developed by Barbara Mann that the Iroquois Confederacy was founded in 1142 A.D. (three centuries earlier than the usual scholarly consensus), George comments that "Some professionals grudgingly acknowledge that the Haudenosaunee (Iroquois) were the most influential indigenous people in North America, yet they dig in their heels at the thought that the Iroquois might have sparked the democratic ideals of the founders of the infant United States."

**1998.028.** Gonzales, Patrisia and Roberto Rodriquez. "Indian Women Are Returning to Their Traditional Leadership Roles." Denver *Post*, July 12, 1998, p. H-3 (Perspective).

This survey of Native American women in leadership roles includes information on the Iroquois Confederacy. "While the Iroquois Confederacy is credited with inspiring the U.S. Constitution, less commonly known is that it was the decisions and words of the women's council that were carried by envoys to...the likes of Benjamin Franklin."

**1998.029.** Gurnett, Kate. "The Many Influences of the Suffrage Movement." Albany *Times Union*, July 5, 1998, p. G-7.

> "If Seneca Falls was a cradle of reform in 1848," writes Gurnett, "it could be said that an Iroquois hand was rocking the cradle. Early suffragists needed to look no further than their Seneca and Onondaga neighbors to witness women active in government and financially independent." This article develops the traditional influence of Iroquois women and their impact on Elizabeth Cady Stanton and Matilda Joslyn Gage, quoting Sally Roesch Wagner. Ten days after this piece was published, Wagner was among scholars of feminism and Iroquois clan mothers who met with First Lady Hillary Clinton as she took part in observations of the Seneca Falls' conference's 150th anniversary. See: Emily Bazar, "Women's Rights: The Fight Goes On." Sacramento *Bee*, July 19, 1998, p. A-1.

**1998.030.** Harris, John F. "Hailing Early Feminists, First Lady Urges Women to 'Finish the Work.'" Washington *Post*, July 17, 1998, p. A-3.

> First Lady Hillary Clinton, who was taking part in activities observing the 150th anniversary of the Seneca Falls conference, on July 15 at Victor, N.Y. (a site the Senecas call Ganondagan) "met with Iroquois clan mothers, discussing how the Iroquois tribes extolled the power of women." This article, a lengthy analysis of Hillary Clinton's role in national politics, goes on to link this meeting with her work on the White House's Millennium Council, a national group planning the future of the Democratic Party, "which is promoting the American past....This week's tour makes clear that the first lady looks to the past as an inspiration for a progressive political and cultural agenda."

**1998.031.** Hipwell, Bill. "Apology Should Have Been a Thank You." *The Financial Post* [Ottawa, Ontario] February 3, 1998, p. 18.

> On January 7, 1998, Canadian Indian Affairs Minister Jane Stewart entered into the record of the House of Commons a "Statement of Reconciliation" apologizing to Canadian natives for historical mistreatment, specifically forced attendance at boarding schools until the 1960s. This statement sparked a retort in the *Financial Post* from columnist David Frum, who wrote, in part: "Let the grovelling begin....The descendants of

the Europeans have had the good taste never to demand a thank-you from the descendants of the aboriginals....But at the very least they are entitled to refuse to bow and scrape and abase themselves for the sin of having tamed and civilized this inhospitable land." This column, published January 13, drew several indignant letters to the editor, one of which was from Bill Hipwell, a lecturer in political geography at Ottawa's Carlton University. Instead of apologizing, Hipwell suggested, Euro-Canadians should thank native peoples for several things, among them democratic ideas: "The civilizations of the Mi'kmaq and the Haudenosaunee (Iroquois) Confederacy [which] taught Europeans such basic principles as human rights....Jefferson borrowed liberally from the Haudenosaunee political system..." Hipwell also provides a quote from Benjamin Franklin ("All their government is by Counsel of Sages...").

**1998.032.** Hipwell, Bill. "Native History Well Researched." *Financial Post* [Ottawa], February 14, 1998, p. 20.

In his second round of debate with *Financial Post* columnist David Frum, Hipwell refutes Frum's assertion (above) that an Iroquois role in the development of democracy is "pure invention." He directs Frum to "Bruce Johansen's *Native American Political Systems and the Evolution of Democracy: An Annotated Bibliography*, which provides scores of scholarly references to the contributions the Haudenosaunee Confederacy made to the U.S. Constitution."

**1998.033.** Holt, Patricia. "Steinem Edits a History of U.S. Women." San Francisco *Chronicle*, April 19, 1998, p. 2. ["Sunday Review"]

Steinem is being interviewed about her editorship of the new *Reader's Companion to Women's History* (1998). Steinem's big discovery in writing this book, she says, "was the realization that the Iroquois Confederacy of six major northeastern tribes 'inspired the structure of the U.S. Constitution, a fact only recently acknowledged in legal history,' its matrilineal society inspired the suffragist movement." Holt's account continues: "'The Iroquois guaranteed the social and political power of women to such an extent," says Steinem, "'That suffragists like Elizabeth Cady Stanton and Susan B. Anthony, who talked and listened to women from the nearby tribes, were able to imagine a life of equality they had never known.'"

**1998.034.** Howard, Diane. "Regas' Creamed Spinach Delicious for Side Dish or Dip." Knoxville *News-Sentinel*, February 11, 1998, p. C-1[Food].

> In the midst of a recipe for creamed spinach served at Regas' Restaurant in Knoxville (and not associated with the recipe by the author) is a short history of the Cherokees, including this sentence: "Thomas Jefferson often cited the Great Law of Peace of the Iroquois Confederacy as a model for the U.S. Constitution."

**1998.035.** Keeler, Jason. [Untitled Letter to the Editor.] Bend [Oregon] *Bulletin*. September 11, 1998, p. E-2.

> Keeler is replying to previous letter in the *Bulletin* which asserts that the U.S. Constitution is based on the *Bible*. Keeler replies that Franklin and Jefferson were Deists, with a very personal view of God, who separated the affairs of church and state. Keeler concludes that the Constitution "is a blend of classical political ideas grafted onto a framework directly inspired (thanks to Benjamin Franklin) by the Great Law of Peace of the League of the Iroquois."

**1998.036.** O'Connor, John. "Bill That Would Remove 'Subjective' Questions from ISAP Advances." Copley News Service, March 11, 1998 (in LEXIS).

> The "ISAP" is the Illinois Goals Assessment Program, a state-wide test for all public-school students, which was being debated in the State Senate. Sen. Patrick O'Malley, Republican of Palos Park, has introduced a bill restricting the types of questions which may be asked on the test. One type of question that may not be asked defines students' self-esteem. In this context, The Rev. Robert Vanden Bosch, director of Concerned Christian-Americans of Lake Zurich, is reported to have objected to a question on the existing state test that "required students to read an essay that contended the U.S. Constitution was based on that of the Iroquois Indian nation, then comment on it." Such a question would not be allowed under Sen. O'Malley's bill.

**1998.037.** Puente, Maria. "Hillary Clinton Commemorates Women's Historic Contributions." *USA Today*, July 16, 1998, p. 2-A.

> Hillary Clinton "sat down for a roundtable of with a group of Iroquois clan mothers in Victor, N.Y.," while in Upstate New York. the same day, she visited The former home of "underground railroad" leader Harriet Tubman.

**1998.038.** Racine, Marty. "Not Enough Warriors: Lawrence Sampson Fought for the U.S.; Now He Fights for His People." Houston *Chronicle*, April 28, 1998, p. 1.

> This front-page feature on Lawrence Sampson, a Delaware and Eastern Cherokee living in Houston, who is also an Army veteran and salesman for a communications firm, asks "How many tribes or Indian nations...existed here before Columbus?...Six hundred. The Cherokees taught Europeans how to build log cabins. The Iroquois Confederacy was the model for the U.S. Constitution."

**1998.039.** Ringe, Jean Pontius. "National Culture Should Recognize Native Culture." Asheville [North Carolina] *Citizen-Times*, September 11, 1998, p. A-11.

> In a letter to the editor, Ringe applauds an editorial in the newspaper which opposed the use of a "squaw" as a mascot at local Erwin High School. It is time to appreciate Native American contributions rather than degrading Native women, Ringe argues. He cites "Ja-gon-sa-seh," the founding mother of the Iroquois Confederation, a constitution "that became, in important ways, a prototype for our own." Ringe describes the Iroquois system at some length, and closes that it would be "nice if Erwin High, and others of us, took note."

**1998.040.** Seabrook, John. "The Gathering of the Tribes: Preppies vs. Indians on an old American Playing Field." *The New Yorker*, September 7, 1998, pp. 30-36.

> This is a profile of lacrosse and, in particular, all-star goalie and coach Oren Lyons. The piece observes on page 30 that the Iroquois "govern themselves through a bicameral system set down in the Iroquois Confederacy's constitution, which was created long before the United States Constitution and is

thought to have influenced both Benjamin Franklin and Thomas Jefferson."

**1998.041.** Weatherford, Jack. "A Look at Making Money: Money Talks. Here's What It Says About Us." Washington *Post* (Outlook), January 4, 1998, p. C-3.

> In a wide-ranging history of coinage, Weatherford notes that Benjamin Franklin designed early United States coins with an Iroquois covenant-chain image: "The Founding Fathers wanted their money to proclaim to the world what their new country stood for -- and to remind its citizens of their country's values. Benjamin Franklin designed the first U.S.. coin, borrowing an emblem from the Iroquois, who used the links of a chain to represent the union of their five nations." This piece also was published in the Minneapolis *Star-Tribune*, the Houston *Chronicle*, and the Denver *Post*.

## *Internet Web Sites*

**1998.042.** Laura Waterman Wittstock. "American Democracy: An Invention or a Discovery?" [http://nnic.com/colors/vol5/amerDemo. html] "Was American democracy invented?" asks Wittstock. "Or did the revolutionists, kicking around to find something different from their historical political roots in England, discover a new way to govern right under their noses?" She describes Iroquois precedents for democracy from the works of Burton (1989), Grinde (1989), and Venables (1989). Wittstock concludes: "The story of democracy, and the Native nations who found themselves hosts to the most misbehaving guests in history, is still unfolding."

**1998.043.** Tim Hundsdorfer. "The Iroquois Confederacy as a Potential Ecofeminist Model." [http://carbon.cudenver.edu/~thundsdo/E-DEM/Iroquois.html] This lengthy paper considers feminist and democratic aspects of the Iroquois political tradition, citing Grinde (I:1977) and Johansen (1982).

**1998.044.** Jack Weatherford. "American Indians: The Original Democrats." *In Context* [http://www.context.org/ICLIB/IC30/Various. htm] "Reportedly, the first person to propose a union of all the colonies and to propose a federal model for it was the Iroquois chief Canassatego, speaking at an Indian-British assembly in Pennsylvania in July 1744. He suggested that they do as his people had done and form a union like the League of the Iroquois."

**1998.045.** Houghton Mifflin Social Studies. Grade 5: "America Will Be." [http://www.eduplace.com/links/hmss/grade5.html] 1998. One listing among many in this bibliography for teachers is "The University of Oklahoma Law Center: The Iroquois Constitution." The Houghton Mifflin Social Studies reading list introduces the listing, which includes the text of the U.S. Constitution and the Iroquois Great Law of Peace, this way: "See how the Iroquois defined their laws, organized their ceremonies, and protected the rights of their people in their Constitution. How is the Constitution of the United States similar to and different from the Iroquois Constitution? To find out, compare the Iroquois Constitution at this site with a copy of the U.S. Constitution."

**1998.046.** Barbara Gray (Kanatiyosh). "The Influence of the Great Law of Peace on the United States Constitution: An Haudenosaunee (Iroquois) Perspective." [http://tuscaroras.com/graydeer/influenc/page1.htm] Barbara Gray (Kanatiyosh) is an Onondaga/Akwesasne Mohawk third-year law student at Arizona State University. Gray compares and contrasts the Great Law Of Peace and the United States Constitution, concluding: "In acknowledging that the Haudenosaunee had a complex centralized government, the Great Law, that was emulated by the founding fathers and existed before the first Europeans arrived, makes the U.S. judicial framework concerning Indians and federal-Indian policy in need of being reexamined and remedied, for no longer can the native peoples be seen as uncivilized and in need of assimilation."

**1998.047.** Syracuse University. "Honors Courses and Seminars: Sophomore Year." [http://sumweb.syr.edu/honors/s98crs.htm] 1998. One of the seminars is: "Haudenosaunee: Historical and Contemporary Issues," Instructor: John Dyer. The course description includes this statement: "The confederate state of the Haudenosaunee became the embodiment of democratic principles which continue to guide our people today. The Haudenosaunee became the first 'United Nations' established on a firm foundation of peace, harmony, and respect."

**1998.048.** David Reilly. "The Compromising of Ideals: The Haudenosaunee and the Genesis of U.S. Political Thought." University of Colorado at Boulder [B.A.] Honors Program Department of Political Science B.A. Honors Thesis Abstract.
[http://ucsub.colorado.edu/~honors/reilly.html]
David Reilly touches on Iroquois constititional influence as he argues in this thesis abstract that: "This...is an attempt to interpret the intentions of the American Founding Fathers in their development of

the U.S. Constitution. It varies from other such analyses in that the basis of consideration is the interaction between the colonial leaders and Native Americans. Native practices and societies, and in particular the Haudenosaunee culture, influenced the Founders and U.S. political roots. In considering the primary sources of American political ideology, the Haudenosaunee society, the European tradition, and the Enlightenment works, it is possible to educe the alternatives available to the Founding Fathers, and subsequently, the decisions they made." This thesis draws the conclusion that the colonial leaders were primarily concerned with the protection of private property: "Ideals were subordinated and compromised to their elite interests. The legacy of the Founders is a system of government that holds property rights to be more sacred than equality, and perpetuates self-interest before the public good."

**1998.049.** "Mrs. Joslyn's Fourth Grade" Wetzel Road Elementary in Liverpool, New York.
[http://www.wre.liverpool.k12.ny.us/WRE/staff/joslyn/joslyn.html]
"We are studying the First Americans in Social Studies. Students have read *The Iroquois*, by Craig and Katherine Doherty as well as sections of their Social Studies text book, *New York Yesterday and Today.* Here is a site we visited during our unit on the First Americans: "The Six Nations: Oldest Living Participatory Government."
[http://www.ratical.com/many_worlds/6Nations/index.html#BCtC]
"This site includes...pictures of the Iroquois: The Tree of Peace, Forgotten Founders, Haudenosaunee Council, and the Longhouse. Students completed a worksheet with this site to show information they had gained. Parents also visited this site with their children. This was an intergenerational learning experience!"

**1998.050.** Sally Roesch Wagner. "Matilda Joslyn Gage: Forgotten Feminist." [http://www.nps.gov/wori/gagebio.htm] under "Created Equal: Women's Rights Historical Park, Seneca Falls." [http://www.nps.gov/wori/wrnhp.htm], re: National Park Service "Parknet" [http://www.nps.gov/index.html]
"Gage, who was adopted into the wolf clan of the Mohawk nation and given the name *Ka-ron-ien-ha-wi* (Sky Carrier), wrote of the superior form of government practiced by the Six Nation Iroquois Confederacy, in which 'the power between the sexes was nearly equal.' This indigenous practice of woman's rights became her vision."

**1998.051.** Summary of Sally Roesch Wagner, *The Untold Story of the Iroquois Influence on Early Feminists.* Sky Carrier Press, 1996.
[http://www.pinn.net/~sunshine/book-sum/wagner2.html]

**1998.052.** Program: 150th Anniversary of the First Women's Rights Convention Women's Rights Historical Park, Seneca Falls, "Special Events." [http://www.nps.gov/wori/celeb98.htm]
June 26: 1 p.m. "The Iroquois Women's Influence on the Women's Rights Movement." Seneca Falls Heritage Area, Visitor Center, 115 Fall Street. Exhibit, reception, and grand opening. Public is invited.

**1998.053.** Office of Intercultural Programs College of St. Benedict, St. John's University Intercultural Resource Center: Native American. [http://www.users.csbsju.edu/~intercul/library/bookna.html]
Review of Bruce E. Johansen, *Forgotten Founders.* "This book traces how the Founding Fathers absorbed American Indian political and social ideas, and how these ideas combined with the cultural heritage they had brought from Europe to create a potential rationale for revolution in the new land. This unique history explains how the organization of Iroquois society, with its egalitarian principles, government by the people, and provisions for the impeachment of erring leaders, impressed the colonists, who incorporated their knowledge of Iroquois culture into the new government, making us all heirs to America's rich Indian heritage."

**1998.054.** Sally Roesch Wagner. "Matilda Joslyn Gage and the Iroquois: An Unknown Feminist-Native American Alliance."
[http://www.nyhistory.com/sallyroeschwagner/mjgiroq.htm]
"The division of power between the sexes in this [Iroquois] Indian republic was nearly equal," Gage wrote. In matters of government, "...its women exercised controlling power in peace and war...no sale of lands was valid without consent of the women, while "the family relation among the Iroquois demonstrated woman's superiority in power...in the home, the wife was absolute...if the Iroquois husband and wife separated, the wife took with her all the property she had brought...the children also accompanied the mother, whose right to them was recognized as supreme...never was justice more perfect, never civilization higher..."

**1998.055.** National Women's History Month Programs Reported For March 1998. [http://www.nwhp.org/reports3.html]
Three new curriculum guides will be available from the Women's Rights National Historical Park, Seneca Falls. One of them is: "Celebrating Your Cultural Heritage: Telling the Untold Stories in Your Community," written by Dr. Sally Roesch Wagner, using as an example in Seneca Falls the influence on the Iroquois women on the early women's rights movement. Contact MaryEllen Snyder, 315-568-2179 or [http://www.MaryEllen_Snyder@nps.gov].

**1998.056.** American Indian Institute [New York, N.Y.] "You're Looking at the First Draft of the Constitution."
[http://www.turan.com/thunderbird/cons.htm]
"Before the ideas of inalienable rights, liberty, and democracy were strung together in words, they were strung together in beads made of shells, in this Iroquois Confederacy wampum belt. It represents 1,000 years of democratic principles that we Indians shared with our newer brothers and sisters. (Including Thomas Jefferson and Benjamin Franklin who openly acknowledged in speeches and in writing that our contribution formed the basis of the Constitution.) We shared our belief that leaders should represent and serve the people. Which was a startling belief in a world of kings and queens. We shared what we call, The Great Law. Which is the natural law of human dignity that precedes and underlies all other laws..." This text is illustrated with a copy of a poster developed by the American Indian Institute which includes a replica of an Iroquois wampum belt over the words: "You're Looking at the First Draft of the Constitution."

**1998.057.** Minneapolis Institute of Arts. "Curriculum Materials: Art in America....Thomas Sully: Portrait of George Washington."
[http://www.artsmia.org/art_in_america/6_5.html]
Text accompanying Sully's portrait of Washington reads, in part: 'Most Euro-American art and oratory of the 19th century associated the new U.S. government with the ancient Roman republic. Despite the stature and prestige attained by this association, the two governments had very little in common. In reality, the writers of the Constitution derived a more significant number of their ideas from the Iroquois Confederacy of Nations, a democratic form of government based on elected representatives. Sully's portrait of Washington, however, includes no reference to the Iroquois Confederacy's contribution.'

**1998.058.** Minnesota Indian Affairs Council. Resources: Teacher Background Information: Tribal Sovereignty.
[http://www.quest-dynamics.com/mniac/s-bkgnd.htm]
"The governments of these nations [Iroquois] have always operated in accordance with democratic principles. An example is the Iroquois Confederacy. The framers of the U.S. Constitution based many of their basic concepts on this confederacy. Each nation within the confederacy selected individuals to represent them at confederacy meetings. Issues were deliberated until all were in agreement on a common course of action. This method of decision-making still used today is called consensus democracy."

**1998.059.** United States Department of Justice. "Address by Attorney General Janet Reno.....United South and Eastern Tribes, Inc., Meeting Arlington, Virginia, Wednesday, February 3, 1998."
[http://www.usdoj.gov/otj/aguset.htm]
Reno's speech includes the following passage: "The framers of our Constitution visited the leaders of the Six Nations Iroquois Confederacy to study the Great Law of Peace. In this way, the wisdom of your elders was made part of our constitutional system of checks and balances. It has been gratifying for me to stand at Harvard Law School, my alma mater, and be taught about the Great Law of Peace in other ways, about what we can do to bring peace amongst our young people."

**1998.60.** Terri Windling. "The Mohawk Vision: Tom Porter on the Legacy of the Millennium." The Millennium Conference, New York City Open Center, November 16-17, 1998. [http://www.omnimag.com/archives/features/millennium/conference/politics.html]
Terri Windling, a science-fiction writer and editor, wrote summary remarks describing a talk by Akwesasne Mohawk leader Tom Porter at a conference on the millennium organized under auspices of *Omni*, a popular-science magazine. Windling points out that the Mohawks were part of the Iroquois Confederacy, who "practiced a democratic form of government...before the U.S. Constitution was written; indeed, Benjamin Franklin was among the admirers who studied the Iroquois Confederacy government 'of the people, for the people, by the people.'"

**1998.61.** Boy Scouts of America. "Index to Merit Badge Requirements."
[http://www.meritbadge.com/bsa/mb/064.htm]
This is one of several web pages that list criteria for the "Indian Lore" merit badge. One of the requirement (as of 1996) is: "Learn about the Iroquois Confederacy, including how and why it was formed. Tell about its governing system, and its importance to the framers of our Constitution of the United States."

## Other Items

**1998.062.** Transcript, Cable News Network, "Talk Back Live," March 12, 1998, 3 p.m. EST, Transcript #98031200V14, in LEXIS. The subject is whether high school students should be required to read "quotas" of books by minority authors. One of the guests, Bonnie Boswell, who is identified as "an advocate of multicultural curricula," remarks that study of minority authors sheds light on familiar subjects. "Most of usdon't know," she said, "that our Constitution was formulated on the basis of the Iroquois nation...[and] Benjamin Franklin."

**1998.063.** Documentary film, "Tree of Peace Society," Nathan Koenig, White Buffalo Multimedia, Woodstock, New York. This fifteen-minute film describes the work of Jake Swamp's Tree of Peace Society, with artwork by John Kahionhes Fadden. The film briefly describes Iroquois governance and its impact on the founders of the United States.

**1998.064.** Cayuga Museum, Auburn, New York, utilized two of John Kahionhes Fadden's posters depicting Iroquois influence on U.S. democracy at an exhibit mounted by Harry Schueler, a German national, during the summer of 1998. The two posters are titled: "Cultural Encounter: The Iroquois Great Law of Peace and the United States Constitution," and "Forgotten Legacy: Native American Concepts and the Formation of United States Government." The first poster was initially developed for the 1987 Cornell University conference on the subject; the second was created for a conference with a similar theme in Philadelphia, for St. Tammany's Day, May 1, 1989.

**1998.065.** Transcript, "Booknotes," National Cable Satellite Corp., May 10, 1998, 8 p.m. Eastern Daylight Time. Arthur Schlesinger, Jr. talks about a new edition of his book, *The Disuniting of America*. In the course of the interview, asked about Iroquois influence on the evolution of democracy, attributes the idea's popularity to "an Iroquois lobby," and special-interest ethnic politics.

**1998.066.** "Iroquois Women: An Inspiration to Early Feminists," invitation to the opening of "Sisters in Spirit: Celebrating the Iroquois Influence on the Early Women's Rights Movement," Traveling Exhibition, at the Urban Cultural Park, Heritage Area, Seneca Falls, New York, June 27, 1998, 4 p.m. Exhibition coordinator: Sally Roesch Wagner.

# 1997

## *Books, Scholarly, and Specialty Publications*

**1997.001.** _____. *The New York Public Library Desk Reference of American History*. New York: Macmillan, 1997.

In a brief biography of Deganawidah, on page 26, this desk

reference notes that "Historians believe [that the Iroquois Confederacy] was one of the models for the United States federal government."

**1997.002.** _____. "Theft of Spirit: From High-priced Sweat Lodges to Imitation Rituals, Native American Spirituality Is Being Debased and Exploited...." *Akwesasne Notes* New Series 2:2(Spring, 1997), pp. 28-30.

> This examination of "new age" spiritual rip-offs of Native American cultures contains a brief description of the Iroquois Confederacy, and its Great Law of Peace, which "fosters the exercise of reason and protects free speech and equality for women, [and] may have been influential in the drafting of the United States Constitution."

**1997.003.** Agel, Jerome. *Words That Make America Great.* New York: Random House, 1997.

> This collection of historical documents includes the text of the Albany Plan (1754) on pages 6 and 7; Agel writes that it was adopted by delegates after Franklin argued for a colonial union that resembled the Iroquois League. In matter of historical fact, Franklin had written that comment in a letter to his printing partner James Parker three years earlier. On page 342, introductory text on "The First Americans" says that Franklin "recommended" the Iroquois Confederacy "as a model" for colonial government. Contrary to this, Pages 345 and 346 contain an excerpt from the Great Law of Peace; an editorial comment says it "was not an influence on the composition of the U.S. Constitution."

**1997.004.** Biolsi, Thomas and Larry J. Zimmerman, eds. *Indians and Anthropologists: Vine Deloria, Jr., and the Critique of Anthropology.* Tucson: University of Arizona Press, 1997.

> This is a book on the evolving relationship between anthropologists and Native Americans, with essays by several different authors, many of whom key their contributions to Vine Deloria, Jr.'s critique of their field of study. The conclusion of the book, "Anthros, Indians, and Planetary Reality," by Deloria himself, includes a detailed description of the controversy over the Iroquois and democracy (pp. 215-217), in which Deloria writes: "This fight over the Six Nations' influence has been a bitter one, and if it had been

submitted to a jury for fair deliberation the anthropological profession would now be paying reparations to the Six Nations, for the evidence and the argument weigh heavily in favor of the Iroquois and their supporters." The "influence" idea also is raised in the context of the New York State curriculum guide Haudenosaunee: *Past, Present, Future* (and the faceoff between traditional Iroquois and anthropological "experts") in Gail Landsman, "Informant as Critic: Conducting Research on a Dispute Between Iroquoianist Scholars and Traditional Iroquois," pp. 160-176. Elisabeth Tooker's article on the subject in *Ethnohistory* (1988) is cited, as is the Johansen-Tooker exchange in the same journal (1990).

**1997.005**. Calloway, Colin G. *New Worlds For All: Indians, Europeans, and the Remaking of Early America.* Baltimore: Johns Hopkins University Press, 1997.

On pages 187-191, Calloway presents a detailed description of the debate over Iroquois precedents for American democracy, citing several works by Grinde, Johansen, and Lyons. He begins with Canassatego's 1744 speech to colonial treaty commissioners urging the English to unite on an Iroquoian model, and continues to Benjamin Franklin's 1751 letter to James Parker advising the same. Although he finds evidence that the Founders "copied" the Constitution from the Iroquois "largely circumstantial and inferential," (p. 188) Calloway lists many ways in which the two systems are similar: "As had the Iroquois, the founding fathers created a system of government where power was distributed and not concentrated, where new tribes or states could join, where authority was derived from the people, where individual freedoms, group autonomy, and freedom of speech were protected..." (p. 188). He also lists ways in which the systems are not similar: the founders did not emphasize the rights of women nor adopt consensus as a governing decisionmaking mechanism. Calloway also describes ways in which the example of the Indian helped shape the new Americans' attitudes toward liberty, from Roger Williams to Franklin: "Indian communities were living proof that human beings could construct and maintain societies based on liberty." (p. 190).

**1997.006.** Ellis, Joseph J. *American Sphinx: The Character of Thomas Jefferson.* New York: Alfred A. Knopf, 1997.

On page 101, Ellis summarizes Jefferson's attitudes toward governmental organization: "There was European society, with governments that ruled by force, usually monarchical in form, what Jefferson described as 'wolves over sheep.' Then there was American, and to slightly lesser extent, English society, with governments responsive to the populace as a whole, where 'the mass of mankind enjoys a precious degree of liberty & happiness.' Finally, there was Indian society, which managed itself without any formal government at all [sic] by remaining small and assuring the internalization of common values among all members." Ellis quotes Jefferson's 1787 letter to Edward Carrington in which he says that "those societies (as the Indians) which live without government enjoy in their gen'l mass an infinitely greater degree of happiness than those who live under European governments."

**1997.007.** Elshtain, Jean Bethke. [Review, Glazer, *We Are All Multiculturalists Now*, 1997] *CivicNet Journal* 1:1 May, 1997, n.p. [Internet: http://www.civicnet.org/journal/issue1/jbethke.htm]

Jean Bethke Elshtain, Laura Spelman Rockefeller Professor of Social and Political Ethics at the University of Chicago, knashes her teeth at length about "political correctness" and "militant multiculturalists' debasement of the standards of scholarship," but by the end of this lengthy review she is calling for presentation of both European and indigenous American precedents for democracy. One wonders what Elshtain really thinks, after saying in one part of this review that "there is not a shred of evidence to back up this claim" that the Iroquois helped shape democracy. Later, she advises historians to explore "federations that emerged independently among a number of the complex indigenous cultures of North America."

**1997.008.** Fraleigh, D.M. and Tuman, J.S. *Freedom of Speech in the Marketplace of Ideas.* New York: St. Martin's Press, 1997.

On page 60, this book addresses "Freedom of Speech in Seventeenth-Century America: Native American Traditions," including an examination of the Iroquois League's extensive use of public opinion in governance, especially provisions directing leaders' skins to be "seven spans thick" to endure public criticism. The authors cite Johansen, *Forgotten Founders* (1982, 1987).

**1997.009.** Glazer, Nathan. *We Are All Multiculturalists Now.* Cambridge, Mass.: Harvard University Press, 1997.

> On page 40, Glazer observes that the New York State *Curriculum of Inclusion* contained mention of the Iroquois' formative role in the development of democracy. Glazer does not seem to know what to make of this. On one hand, he writes, based on what he has read, the Iroquois role is "insignificant, perhaps nonexistent." On the other hand Glazer seems to realize that he hasn't read much, since he cites no sources, for or against.

**1997.010.** Griffen, Robert and Donald A. Grinde. Jr., *Apocalypse de Chiokoykikoy: Chief of the Iroquois.* Laval, Quebec: Laval University Press, 1997.

> This is the text of a propaganda booklet prepared by American patriots during the Revolutionary War. It was prepared in America, but published in France, and uses Iroquois imagery. This book is the first publication of this tract in English; it contains both French and English texts on opposite pages. *Exemplar of Liberty* (1991) is cited.

**1997.011.** Grinde, Donald A., Jr. and Bruce E. Johansen. [Letter to the Editor] *William and Mary Quarterly,* 3rd ser. Vol. LIV, No. 2, (1997), pp. 469-472.

> Grinde and Johansen reply to assertions against the Iroquois influence thesis by Timothy Shannon in the same issue (below).

**1997.012.** Hagstrom, Mike. "Dr. Johansen Honored by Colleagues." *CommUNO News,* Summer, 1997, p. 3.

> This piece in the alumni newsletter of the Communication Department at the University of Nebraska at Omaha details local reaction to Johansen's winning of the university's annual award for outstanding research and creative activity in May, 1997.

**1997.013.** Hayes, Robert G. *A Race at Bay: New York Times Editorials on the "Indian Problem."* Carbondale: Southern Illinois University Press, 1997.

> In an editorial ("The Six Nations," June 28, 1873), the *New York*

*Times* described the Iroquois League and its political system, including this sentence: "...[T]hey generally organized for themselves a substantial reproduction of the Achaean League, or, more strictly, an anticipation of our own national confederacy." (Hayes, 329) In a second editorial (page 346 in Hayes, July 11, 1893 in the newspaper), the *Times* notes that several Iroquois chiefs have arrived to represent the Six Nations at the Chicago World's Fair. The editorial then describes the Iroquois' political system as a high order of federalism, and criticizes contemporary scholars of government for ignoring the Iroquois example when they ascribe the origins of federalism only to Greek models.

**1997.014.** Hoshikawa, Jun. *Pacific Rim Innernet Journeys: Wisdom of the Mongoloid Indigenous Peoples.* Tokyo: NTT Publishing, 1997. [in Japanese]

Hoshikawa, who traveled widely in North America during the 1990s, describes indigenous cultures of the Pacific Rim and North America. One of his chapters is on the Iroquois Confederacy, titled "Native Roots of Freedom." The chapter (pp. 103-162) discusses Iroquois contributions to democratic ideas in depth, and cites, among other works, Grinde and Johansen, *Exemplar of Liberty*, Barreiro, *Indian Roots of Democracy*, articles by Sally Roesch Wagner, and books by Jack Weatherford.

**1997.015.** Hoxie, Frederick. "Ethnohistory in a Tribal World." *Ethnohistory* 44:4(Fall, 1997), pp. 595-616.

Hoxie mulls what he calls a "contributionist" school of thinking, in which authors stress the role a group played in an historical process -- Native Americans in the evolution of democracy, for example. Critiquing Jack Weatherford's writings, Hoxie glances a brief blow off the "influence" issue, quoting in tidbits from Johansen's reply to Tooker in *Ethnohistory* (1990). From this scanty sample, Hoxie then speculates about Johansen's state of mind: "Nowhere in this argument is there a sense that influences on American or Iroquoian culture are fluid, multifaceted, unexpected, and unpredictable." Hoxie then classifies his mental picture of Johansen's work as an "essentialist version of ethnohistorical materials."(p. 603) This article is derived from Hoxie's presidential address at an annual meeting of the American

Society for Ethnohistory.

**1997.016.** Jemison, G. Peter, curator. *Where We Stand: Contemporary Haudenosaunee Artists.* Catalogue for showing at Fenimore House Museum, New York State Historical Association, August 15 - December 21, 1997, unpaginated.

> In the course of his introductory statement for this catalogue, Jemison writes: "The Haudenosaunee have had a profound influence upon the American public, first with our democratic form of government, and the exchanges between our chiefs and individuals, including Benjamin Franklin and Thomas Jefferson. Later, the women who founded the voting-rights movement were influenced by Onondaga and Oneida women when they witnessed their freedom."

**1997.017.** Jenkins, Philip. *A History of the United States.* New York: St. Martin's Press, 1997.

> On page 59, while discussing the adoption of a two-house legislature in the United States Constitution, Jenkins writes that the structure of the Senate "owed something to the practice of the Iroquois Confederation, in which each tribe held one vote regardless of size." Jenkins also attributes influence to the English parliamentary system as well, seeing the result as a synthesis.

**1997.018.** Lyons, Oren (Jong Quisho). "Epilogue: Opening Remarks, The Year of the Indigenous Peoples, Oka Revisited," in Andrea P. Morrison and Irwin Cotler, eds. *Justice for Natives: Searching for Common Ground.* Montreal: McGill-Queens University Press, 1997, pp. 298-312.

> This is a transcript of several conferences at McGill-Queen's University Law School, held following the confrontation at Oka in 1990. The conferences were a retrospective on the situation at Oka and a forum on Canadian native rights in general. In an appendix, Oren Lyons discusses the formation and operations of the Iroquois Confederacy's political system, including, on page 304, statements that the "fledgling United States government" took shelter under the Great Tree of Peace. "So...the democratic principles [of the Iroquois] are really the fundamental basis of the government of the United States."

**1997.019.** Magill, Frank N. *Great Events From History: North American Series*, Revised Ed. Pasadena, Calif.: Salem Press, 1997.

> The use of the American Indian as a symbol of colonial liberty is mentioned in "1773: Boston Tea Party," citing Grinde and Johansen, *Exemplar of Liberty* (1991). See also: "1500: Iroquois Confederacy," "1754: Albany Congress," and "1776: Indian Delegation Meets with Congress."

**1997.020.** Morrison, Dane, ed. *American Indian Studies: An Interdisciplinary Approach to Contemporary Issues.* New York: Peter Lang, 1997.

> In the first chapter of this book (p. 9), Morrison assails the "influence" idea, and advises "professional historians" to steer clear of it. "Popular writers make the claim that the U.S. Constitution was based on the system of the Iroquois Confederacy. Their assertion rests on the 'fact' that Benjamin Franklin and other colonial leaders held treaty negotiations with the Iroquois during the 1750s, and these same leaders helped draw up the Constitution....This is one example of how a story can be oversimplified when the writer neglects to study evidence of the past." Morrison is leveling this charge at Donald Grinde, whose *Iroquois and the Founding of the American Nation* (1977) is his only cited source in favor of the idea.

**1997.021.** Nash, Gary B. "Early American History and the National History Standards." *William and Mary Quarterly* Third Ser. Vol. 54, No. 3, July, 1997, pp. 579-600.

> Gary B. Nash, professor of history at UCLA, reviews the public debate over national history standards in which he played a central role, including, on pp. 592-594, different viewpoints regarding to what degree Europe's history, including ideas of democracy, was shaped by Native American and African influences. Nash shares some of his personal correspondence with such intellectual celebrities as Arthur Schlesinger, Jr. and Diane Ravitch, as well as the gutterwailings of Rush Limbaugh and other very public critics of notions that Native Americans and Africans shaped the ideological history of Europeans and their descendants around the world.

**1997.022.** Oppenheimer, Mark. "Tribal Lore." *Lingua Franca: The Review of Academic Life.* March, 1997, pp. 8-9.

> Oppenheimer quotes extensively from the 1996 forum in *William and Mary Quarterly,* with a definite anti-"influence" bias. He writes of the idea that "Fancy is a wily seductress," and ends with a string of quotes discrediting the idea from James Axtell, Wilcomb Washburn, and Daniel K. Richter, concluding that "the scholarly community is unswayed by the reply," referring to Grinde and Johansen's case. "The most usable past," concludes Oppenheimer, "may be the real one."

**1997.023.** Salins, Peter D. *Assimilation, American Style.* San Francisco: New Republic/HarperCollins, 1997.

> Page 90: "As Americans were differentiating themselves from their nominal or actual English ancestors in the realm of ideas, attitudes, and values, whatever remained of English cultural influences was also being progressively diluted by their contact with an ever-expanding array of non-English peoples. First, the European settlers were changed by contact with the real 'native' Americans...who introduced them to new foods, new arts and crafts, new modes of shelter, new strategies for survival in the wilderness, and perhaps even some important civic principles." Salins cites Richard Bernstein, *Dictatorship of Virtue* (1994).

**1997.024.** Schmidt, Alvin J. *The Menace of Multiculturalism.* Westport, Conn.: Praeger, 1997.

> Schmidt, a professor of sociology at Illinois College, Jacksonville, is an opponent of multiculturalism who takes no prisoners. On pages 43 and 44, at the beginning of a chapter titled "The Facts Be Damned," he lists a number of facts that he says multiculturalists have "invented." One of these is that "the Constitution of the United States was shaped by the Iroquois Indians." He also slams the idea that Crispus Attucks, the first casualty of the Boston Massacre, was black (He was only half black. The other half of his ancestry was American Indian.) Schmidt says that the "influence" idea is "undocumented." Schmidt would rather history stress the cruel and violent aspects of Native American cultures, which he says squishy-soft multiculturalists downplay. Schmidt is barely getting warmed up. Later in the book, he argues that American

Indian cultures were environmentally destructive and that women in native societies lived "in virtual slavery." On pp. 52 and 53, Schmidt returns to the "influence" issue, calling it a "fabrication." He also asserts that multiculturalists exaggerate the role of Iroquois women. Elsewhere, the author calls the Iroquois influence idea "historical fiction."

**1997.025.** Shannon, Timothy J. [Letter to the editor] *William and Mary Quarterly*, 3rd ser. Vol. LIV, No. 2, pp. 467-469.

Shannon challenges assertions in support of the Iroquois influence thesis by Grinde and Johansen in *WMQ*, Summer, 1996 [below].

**1997.026.** Sonnie, Amy. "Sally Roesch Wagner: Reconstructing Women's History." *Listen Up!* [Voices From the Syracuse University Women's Collective]. Spring, 1997, pp. 4-5.

This article describes Wagner's research and lectures at Syracuse University during the Spring of 1997, when she held a distinguished visiting professorship there. The article notes that Wagner is working on a book titled *Is Equality Indigenous?* which "focuses on...the Iroquois' influence on early feminism."

**1997.027.** Starna, William A. [Review, Venables, *The Six Nations of New York: The 1892 United States Extra Census Bulletin.*] *Ethnohistory* 44:3(Summer, 1997), pp. 579-581.

Starna believes that students of the Iroquois will appreciate having the 1892 *Census Bulletin* in print, but he thinks the Introduction by Venables is "weak." One of several things that stick in Starna's legendary craw about the Introduction is the fact that Venables "uses this opportunity to promote the tired claim of Iroquois influence on the Founding Fathers."

**1997.028.** Tillyard, Stella. *Citizen Lord: Edward Fitzgerald (1763-1798)*, London: Chatto Publishers, 1997.

*Citizen Lord: Edward Fitzgerald (1763-1798)* describes the life of an Irish aristocrat who studied Rousseau, and then traveled to America as a high-ranking officer in the British Army. In America, Fitzgerald was adopted by the Iroquois, which he used as examples in his advocacy of an egalitarian state, especially the abolition of primogeniture. Returning from

America and the Iroquois, Fitzgerald witnessed the early days of the French Revolution, then returned to Ireland to advance the cause of complete human equality in rights and property. Fitzgerald died in a Dublin jail at age 35 in 1798 following an abortive Irish uprising against British rule. He died slowly and painfully of a gunshot wound sustained during the rebellion; the British denied him medical treatment to spare themselves the embarrassment of putting him on trial.

**1997.029.** Tilton, Robert S. [Review, Hauptman, *Tribes and Tribulations* (1995)] *American Historical Review* 102:1(February, 1997), pp. 177-178.

In a favorable review, Tilton notes that "in the third essay he critiques the widely held (and widely taught) belief that the framers of the Constitution looked to the Iroquois Confederacy as a model by pointing out that James Wilson's ideas can be traced more clearly to Montesquieu than to the Iroquois."

**1997.030.** Underwood, Paula. *Franklin Listens When I Speak: Tellings of the Friendship Between Benjamin Franklin and Skenandoah, an Oneida Chief.* San Anselmo, Calif.: A Tribe of Two Press, 1997.

The idea that the Iroquois shaped democracy in the United States is raised briefly in several places in this book (jacket, frontpiece, pp. 106, 107, 115). Most of the book is a prose poem purportedly linking the author to the bloodlines of both Franklin and Skenandoah -- quite a notable assertion, because the two men share no other known ancestors.

**1997.031.** White, Richard. [Review, Colin G. Calloway, *New Worlds for All*] *American Historical Review* 102:5(December, 1997), pp. 1558-59.

Richard White, professor of history at the University of Washington, observes that Calloway's book describes how Native Americans and European-American immigrants interacted on the frontier. "In arena after arena [they] traded, fought, negotiated, intermarried, and exchanged ideas and material practices." (p. 1559) White seems sometimes to wonder whether Calloway treads too often on ground explored by what he calls "the contributionist school of Jack Weatherford's popular histories, in which culture seems to be a list of discrete things and practices to be borrowed by one group from another." (p. 1559). In the end, however, White concludes that Calloway is "cautious and careful not to claim too much." (p. 1559)

**1997.032.** Williams, Robert A., Jr. *Linking Arms Together: American Indian Treaty Visions of Law and Peace, 1600-1800.* New York: Oxford University Press, 1997.

> In a long footnote (pp. 171-172), legal scholar Robert A. Williams, Jr. says that in this book he has "assiduously tried to avoid...overt engagement in the academic debate about the degree of influence of American Indian political ideas on the Founders of the United States and the drafting of the Constitution of 1787." Williams then lists a number of sources on the debate, pro and con, and writes that "American Indian visions of law and peace...are worthy of serious study."

## Newspapers, Magazines, and Newsletters

**1997.033.** _____. "Performance Features Portrayal of Suffragist." *UIS* [University of Illinois at Springfield] *Weekly*, March 17, 1997.

> Announcement of a March 26 performance in character of Matilda Joslyn Gage by Sally Roesch Wagner, at the Studio Theatre, University of Illinois at Springfield. The article also notes that Wagner will give an additional lecture on "The Indigenous Roots of Feminism."

**1997.034.** _____. "Feminist Scholar to Speak at UVM." Burlington [Vermont] *Free Press*, February 26, 1997, p. 1-B.

> Announcement of a lecture by Sally Roesch Wagner, "Native American Roots of Feminism," at 3:30 p.m. February 26 at the University of Vermont. This lecture was coordinated by Donald A. Grinde, Jr., director of ethnic studies and professor of history there.

**1997.035.** _____. "Internet Stops: Firecracker Path to History Lights Way to Forefathers." Seattle *Times*, June 29, 1997, p. C-2.

> This is a listing of Internet sites, compiled by the staff of Excite

(the Web search engine), including "Key Documents in American History," listing, according to this article, "documentation of the democratic process from the Magna Carta to the 27th Amendment of the U.S. Constitution.... Classics such as the Bill of Rights...Articles of Confederation, Annapolis Convention, Mayflower Compact and Iroquois Constitution."
[http://ucsbuxa.ucsb.edu:3001/11/.stacks/.historical]

**1997.036.** _____. "The Unknown Constitution" [Editorial] *Investor's Business Daily*, September 17, 1997, p. A-34.

This editorial begins with the results of a survey of 1,000 adults disclosing that many do not know the basics of the U.S. Constitution. According to this piece, 48 per cent knew the number of senators (100), and 58 per cent knew the three branches of the federal government, while only 34 per cent knew that the first ten amendments to the Constitution are called the Bill of Rights. The editorial then adds, with no statistical support: "Given today's teaching methods and textbook biases, we'd guess that few high-school seniors know about impeachment powers, while most are convinced that the framers of the Constitution got their ideas from the Iroquois League of Nations." The operative word here is "guess."

**1997.037.** _____. "Word by Word. Linguist Works to Preserve an American Indian Language." University of Southern California *Times*, reprinted in *Huron Newsletter*, November 23, 1997.

Bruce L. Pearson, an emeritus professor of linguistics at USC, has received a $300,000 grant from the Department of Health and Human Services to develop a handbook and dictionary of the Wyandot (Huron) language. Asked why he is doing this, Pearson replied that the language needs to be preserved, in part, because "American Indian history and heritage is part of the heritage of all Americans....'We tend to assume that our governmental institutions were developed from European institutions, when in fact Europe was dominated by monarchies, and our own Constitution is in many ways much closer to the League of the Iroquois and other democratic institutions....Benjamin Franklin, in particular, was impressed by this league and his writings speak of it as a model for the system of American government.'"

**1997.038.** Axtell, James. "Paddling Their Own Canoes." [Review, Calloway, *New Worlds for All*] *London Times Literary Supplement*, June 6, 1997.

> Axtell is reviewing a new book, Colin Calloway's *New Worlds for All: Indians, Europeans, and the Remaking of America* (Baltimore: John Hopkins University Press). In this review, Axtell expresses approval of the argument that Native Americans influenced European-Americans in many ways, but not in the development of democracy. Axtell praises Calloway for avoiding the "trap" of making such a point, which he characterizes as "wishful thinking...of those who have argued that the U.S. Constitution was modelled on the Iroquois Confederacy."

**1997.039.** Bedy, Zoltan. "Feminist Pioneer Named Visiting Scholar." *Syracuse Record*, January 21, 1997, p. 2.

> This piece in the house organ of the Syracuse University administration describes the appointment of Sally Roesch Wagner as a visiting distinguished professor in women's studies: "Wagner is a feminist historian who has done extensive research on [Matilda Joslyn] Gage, and other areas of feminism, particularly as it has been influenced by Native American thought."

**1997.040.** Conklin, Bernie. "Halbritter Sticks His Foot in His Mouth." [Letter to the Editor] Oneida *Daily Dispatch*, May 8, 1997, p. 4.

> As part of a debate over the lack of democracy in the regime of Ray Halbritter, elected tribal chairman of the New York Oneidas, Conklin wrote: "...The Iroquois Confederacy had a democratic government of the people, by the people, and for the people long before Europeans came to this country."

**1997.041.** Harrison-Brighton, Regina. "Jacoby's Portrait of Indians was Wrong." [Letter to the Editor] Boston *Globe*, October 13, 1997, p. A-14.

> Harrison is replying to an op-ed piece headlined "Christopher Columbus Deserves to be Admired," in the *Globe* (October 9, 1997), which also was distributed by the New York *Times* news service and published in several other newspapers. Harrison,

who writes that she studied the Iroquois Confederacy for five years in graduate school, says that "Jacoby's characterization of the Indians of the Americas as savage cannibals without morals is inaccurate." She offers, in refutation, the Iroquois story of the Peacemaker. In addition, Harrison writes, "Benjamin Franklin and Thomas Jefferson spoke of their admiration for the political system and the social mores of the Iroquois."

**1997.042.** Harman, Claire. "Playing at Revolution; *Citizen Lord: Edward Fitzgerald* by Stella Tillyard, Chatto... [Book review], *The Independent* [London, England], May 18, 1997, p. 18.

**1997.043.** Hillaire, Darrell. "Sovereignty is Unity of Purpose, Clarity of Mind." *Indian Country Today*, May 5-12, 1997, p. A-5.

Hillaire, vice chairman of the Lummi Nation (Washington State), surveys legal concerns related to Native American sovereignty, noting that the United States and Native American nations had a peer relationship when the U.S. Constitution was adopted, a fact that helped shape the character of U.S. government through diplomatic interaction: "The Iroquois Confederacy provided a model for the Founding Fathers in drafting the U.S. Constitution. Immediately after the Declaration of Independence, the Continental Congress sent ambassadors to the Indian nations."

**1997.044.** Johansen, Bruce E. "The Iroquois: Present at the Birth." *Wall Street Journal* [Letter to the editor], April 10, 1997, p. A-15.

Johansen is replying to a review by Afrocentricism critic Mary Lefkowitz (below). He asserts that giving credit to the Iroquois does not demean classical Greek or English precedents for United States basic law, but "simply add[s] an Iroquois role to the picture." He concludes: "We can have our Greeks, and our Iroquois, too."

**1997.045.** Johansen, Bruce E. "Reprise of Iroquois 'Influence' Issue." *Native Americas* 14:2(Summer, 1997), pp. 58-60.

This is a sometimes satirical rebuttal to various abject denials of Iroquois influence on democracy, with special attention to Robert Bork's *Slouching Toward Gomorrah: The Decline of*

*American Liberalism,* as well as other similarly visceral reactions against the "influence" idea.

**1997.046.** Johansen, Bruce E. "Politically Pluribus." *Omaha Magazine,* July / August, 1997, p. 61.

Johansen debates multicultural education, including the Iroquois contribution to democracy, with Doug Kagan, Nebraska state chairman of the Nebraska Conservatives for Freedom, in their bimonthly point-counterpoint column in *Omaha Magazine.*

**1997.047.** Laduke, Winona. "Rights We Need to Protect: We Need an Amendment to Protect the Environment." *News and Record* [Greensboro, N.C.] July 4, 1997.

Winona LaDuke, a Native American environmental activist, proposes that a constitutional amendment protecting the environment be adopted, as is "reflected in the Iroquois Confederacy's philosophy: We must consider the impact of a decision made today on the seventh generation from now." The same piece was published in the Bergen, New Jersey, *Record,* also on July 4, 1997.

**1997.048.** Lefkowitz, Mary. "Out of Many, More Than One." *Wall Street Journal,* March 24, 1997, p. A-16.

This is a review of *The Menace of Multiculturalism* (by Alvin J. Schmidt) and *We Are All Multiculturalists Now,* by Nathan Glazer. The review begins: "Does the U.S. Constitution owe more to the 18th-century Iroquois than it does to the ancient Greeks? No, but many younger people may answer yes, because it is what they have learned in school. The history that children learn is not necessarily a record of what actually happened in the past; rather, it is often an account of what parents and teachers believe they ought to know." Later in the review, Lefkowitz, a professor of classics at Wellesley College, writes that "however impressive the governmental organization of the Iroquois nation, the inspiration behind the Constitution may once again be credited to the European Enlightenment, and the ancient Greeks." Lefkowitz is the author of *Not Out of Africa,* a widely-quoted critique of Afrocentric education.

**1997.049.** Lowen, J. Trout. "The Iroquois-Suffragist Connection: Researcher Says Native American Women Helped Steer 1800s Equal Rights Agenda." Syracuse *Herald-American*, April 6, 1997, pp. AA-1, AA-5.

> This article, which occupied the top half of the "Central New York" section page in the Sunday *Herald-American*, includes a lengthy description of Sally Roesch Wagner's recent work regarding the influence of Iroquois women on nineteenth-century feminists, especially Matilda Joslyn Gage. Wagner at the time was finishing a distinguished visiting professorship in women's studies at Syracuse University. Lowen writes that "Wagner believes Iroquois women had a powerful influence on the women's rights movement, and on the seemingly utopian society that [Elizabeth Cady] Stanton, [Lucretia] Mott, and Gage envisioned when they penned the Declaration of Sentiment, a virtual call to arms, in 1848." This declaration was a convening document of the Seneca Falls conference that heralded the beginnings of organized feminism in the United States. The article says that Wagner relates her work to assertions that the Iroquois also helped shape the ideological corpus of democracy in the United States during the previous century.

**1997.050.** Matz, George. "'Indian Country' Decisions Offer Chance to Reinvent Democracy." Anchorage *Daily News*, June 1, 1997, p. 4G.

> In an op-ed column, Anchorage freelance writer George Matz comments on plans by the state of Alaska to spend up to $1 million to appeal a decision by the Ninth Circuit Court of Appeals that Venetie, an Alaskan Native village, is part of "Indian Country." Matz questions the legal attempt to bring Venetie into the state "melting pot." As he makes his case, Matz describes the Iroquois Confederacy and Benjamin Franklin's appreciation of its governmental system, citing Jack Weatherford's *Indian Givers*. Matz says that he has visited 70 Native villages in Alaska and found people in most of them to "have an innate sense of democracy." Rather than trying to impose "democracy" on Native Alaskans from the outside, Matz implies that other Alaskans should learn from them.

**1997.051.** Meany, Helen. "A Hero for the Times: *Citizen Lord: Edward Fitzgerald (1763-1798)*," [Book review] *Irish Times* [Dublin], April 19, 1997, Weekend Supplement, p. 8.

**1997.052.** Penkava, Melinda. "Democracy." [Transcript, National Public Radio, "Talk of the Nation,"], July 3, 1997, 2 p.m. EDT.

> The subject of the July 3, 1997 edition of NPR's "Talk of the Nation" was "Democracy," in keeping with the eve of Independence Day. During the course of the show, a caller, "Fred," from Minneapolis, asked "Why is it never mentioned -- the contributions that American Indians and tribal governments and specifically the Iroquois Confederacy have made to the Declaration [of Independence] as well as the Constitution of the United States....I've read numerous times the listing of these contributions..." Pauline Maier, author of *American Scripture: Making the Declaration of Independence*, replied "I don't know of any effort or any evidence that Indian examples in any way fed into the Declaration of Independence. There is, however, and has been, a substantial amount of attention to the possible [influence of] the example of the Iroquois on the Constitution." Joseph Ellis, author of *American Sphinx: The Character of Thomas Jefferson* [see above], also replied: "There's been a lively scholarly controversy about the relevance of the Iroquois Confederacy on political models....[T]he bulk of the evidence suggests that it's more limited than some of the most fervent advocates would want it to be. That said, Jefferson used to talk a lot about the Indian form of government himself as a kind of utopian ideal."

**1997.053.** Schlafly, Phyllis. "National Standards Mean National Control." Copley News Service, September 9, 1997.

> In the context of President Clinton's proposal for national school standards, Schlafly, a long-time critic of feminism, complains that politics have ruined the application of national standards for the teaching of U. S. history. Her first assertion of support for this idea is: "A high school social studies teacher told me that three new social-studies textbooks all pay homage to the new gods of multiculturalism by teaching that we got our Constitution from the Iroquois Indians."

**1997.054.** Sleeper, Jim. [Book review: Nathan Glazer, *We Are All Multiculturalists Now*] *New York Times Book Review*, April 27, 1997, Sec. 7, p. 37.

"Instead of taking on multiculturalism or addressing the African-American condition, Mr. Glazer spends chapters asserting that even some fantastical multicultural notions are with us to stay. He doubts that Native Americans helped shape the Constitution. 'But how important is it that students should know that,' he asks. If teaching that the Hodenosaunee federation influenced the Founding Fathers is a way of raising 'Native Americans in the esteem of their fellow students, would that be a justification' for including the story in the curriculum? He never decides."

**1997.055.** Yardley, Jonathan. "Lament For A Common Culture." *Washington Post Book World*, March 16, 1997, p. X0-3.

In an otherwise laudatory review of Nathan Glazer's *We Are All Multiculturalists Now* [Harvard University Press, 1996], Yardley scores Glazer for coming "dangerously close to endorsing bad history -- the ostensible influence of the Iroquois on the framers of the U.S. Constitution, for example." He cites the idea as an example of multiculturalism as "mere feel-good amateur therapy." In an attempt to be sympathetic to Indians in this regard, Yardley says that Glazer "falls over backwards."

## *Internet Web Sites*

**1997.056.** [http://www. wsu. edu.8080/ ~dee /Iroquois League. html] contains a brief description of the Iroquois League and its origins, adding: "This would become the model for the framers of the Constitution."

**1997.057.** [http://www.i-magine.com/wbunge/content.html]; a monograph of unlisted authorship which contains a Marxist analysis of Iroquois matriarchy, quoting liberally from Frederich Engels' *Origin of the Family, Private Property, and the State* [1886].

**1997.058.** http://freenet.Buffalo.edu/lib/shrine/Iroq.html; Advocates an Iroquois influence on the U.S. Constitution, citing Charles Mee, *Genuis of the People* [1987], regarding John Rutledge's use of Iroquois political language while serving on the Committee of Detail at the Constitutional Convention.

**1997.059.**  Blue Mountain Arts (a greeting-card company), utilizes *Forgotten Founders* (1982, 1987) in a page on "Native American Contributions," including a history "Trivia Quiz" with questions such as "Who advised Benjamin Franklin in 1744 to unite the colonists into a confederacy?" [ http://www.bluemountainarts.com/eng/nativeamer/ Native Amer.html ]

**1997.060.**  *Exemplar of Liberty* was cited in "Haudenosaunee Council," by John Kahionhes Fadden; Internet: http://www.ratical.com/many-worlds/6nations.html.    *Forgotten Founderes* was cited in "The Six Nations: The Oldest Living Participatory Democracy on Earth;" Internet [http://www.ratical.com/many-worlds/6nations.html]    "The Iroquois Legacy;"  [http://hank.hama-med.ac.jp/dbk/iroquois.html] also mentions the influence of the Iroquois League on the founders of the United States.

**1997.061.**  Devin Bent.  "The Haudenosaunee (Iroquois) Confederation: Background and Political Correctness." Political Science Department, James Madison University, 1997.
[http:www.jmu.edu/polisci/madison/Iroquois.htm]
Devin Bent, chairman of the Political Science Department at James Madison University, has authored a large number of Internet home pages about James Madison's political life.  On one of these, he describes the Iroquois Confederacy, and then somewhat ambivalently touches on the debate regarding Iroquois influence on the evolution of the United States.  He says that there is "little evidence that the founding fathers ever read the Haudenosaunee Constitution." To do so would have been a remarkable feat, since even a summary of the Great Law was not translated into English until the nineteenth century. Bent writes, quoting Charles Beard, that the Founders were men rich "in political experience, and in practical knowledge....Many had met, fought, negotiated, and traded with the Six Nations and other Native Americans for much of their lives."  Bent concludes that "It seems unlikely that the Founders could be totally blind to the lessons to be learned from the successes and failures of the Six Nations."  Bent's piece is woefully short on specific history.  He fails to mention, among other things, Madison's travels to Iroquois country.

**1997.062.**  Press Release, Kalamazoo College, October 1, 1997, by John Greenhoe, "Sally Roesch Wagner Presents Performance, Lecture on Women's Rights.  Wagner will speak at Kalamazoo College October 17 on, among other subjects, "Iroquois Influence on White Women's Rights." The press release says that Wagner "maintains...that Iroquois society has provided, and still does, a model for women's rights...which were notably absent from the experiences of white women in the nineteenth century." [Internet:http://www.max.cs.kzoo.edu/~ckemeny/press/100197B.html]

**1997.063.** *Forgotten Founders* was reviewed in "American Indians: What's Hot...Links to Native American Nations."
[http://www.geocities.com/Yosemite/8814/Thirdpage.htm]

**1997.064.** Harry V. Martin. "How Indians Helped Create the U.S. Constitution." [http://freeamerica.com/indians.html]
Remarks Martin: "History would have you believe that the new American government was formed from democratic principles supplied by European nations. Yet, every European nation was under the dictatorial powers of an absolute monarch in some form, and the concept of democracy was never part of the practice of Europe in the 1700s....What institutions could they copy from?...The unique concept of democracy -- true democracy -- was found on tiny islands, in the eastern woods of the continent, on the plains and the prairies. Democracy existed before Columbus, before Richard the Lion Heart, before the Magna Carta -- it existed on the shores of a land unknown to the Western World for a thousand years." Martin then describes the Iroquois Confederacy, quoting extensively from Weatherford, *Indian Givers* (1988). Martin quotes Weatherford as saying: "Modern democracy, as we know it today, is as much the legacy of the American Indians, particularly the Iroquois and the Algonquians, as it is of the British settlers, of French political theory, or of all the failed efforts of the Greeks and Romans."

**1997.065.** Oyate [A Native collective in California] "High School and Up" reading list. [http://indy4.fdl.cc.mn.us/~oyate/adult.html]
This reading list includes José Barreiro, ed., *Indian Roots of American Democracy.* 1992, and introduces it this way: "The Great Law of Peace of the Haudenosaunee Confederacy, which united five nations, provided a basis for diplomacy, and differed in many ways from the system of government familiar to the colonists. Benjamin Franklin and others incorporated its principles and symbols into what later became the U.S. Constitution. This book fills in what the textbooks have left out."

**1997.066.** Sally Roesch Wagner's "Is Equality Indigenous: The Untold Story of Iroquois Influence on Early Radical Feminists" was a required reading in Sociology 890 (Feminist Methodologies), Prof. Marjorie DeVault, Syracuse University, Spring, 1997.
[http://web.maxwell.syr.edu/maxpages/special/socweb/syl_s97/890.htm]

**1997.067.** Tidewater, Virginia, National Organization For Women. *NOW or Never* [newsletter]. November, 1997. "Feminist Foremothers: Native American Women." Review of Sally Roesch Wagner, *The Untold Story of the Iroquois Influence on Early Feminists* (Sky Carrier Press) [http://www.now-va.org/chapters/tidewate/newsletr/nov97. html#4moms] "In short, Wagner concludes that Stanton and Gage transcended patriarchy because they had first-hand experience with an egalitarian society. Many thanks to our Native American feminist foremothers for the example which they gave to our 19th century feminist theoreticians."

**1997.068.** Loretta Kemsley. "Matriarch: An Iroquois Celebration of Womanhood." Interview with Oneida singer Joanne Shenandoah about her new recording, "Matriarch."
[http://www.moondance.org/Autumn97/Nonfiction/shenando.htm]
"Joanne Shenandoah's newest album, her sweet vocals rising as softly as the mist. Spirit, time, and earth are woven together into a tapestry which fills the soul with the gentle pride of being female, of surviving life's travails, of our blessings of age, wisdom, and strength....The Haudenosaunee originated unique political ideals such as those of civil cooperation which influenced the creation of the federal government of the United States. In seeking a model for their new confederation, Benjamin Franklin and Thomas Jefferson sought the counsel of Haudenosaunee elders and based their version of democratic ideals upon this knowledge."

**1997.069.** Joe Byrd [Principal Chief] and James "Garland" Eagle [Deputy Principal Chief]. Home page, the Cherokee Nation, Tahlequah, Oklahoma. [http://www.cherokee.org/constit.htm]
This home page of the Cherokee Nation of Oklahoma begins: "O-si-yo: At least 300 years prior to the passage of the United States Constitution, American democracy began with the Iroquois Confederacy's Law of the Great Peace. The Cherokee belong to the Iroquois language family of eastern North America, which includes five related tribes comprising the Iroquois Confederacy. The representative democracy of the Iroquois was extensively studied and praised by Benjamin Franklin and Thomas Jefferson, who often referred to it as the basis for the United States Constitution." This statement precedes the 1975 version of the Cherokee Constitution.

## Other item

**1997.070.** Documentary film, "Oren Lyons, Faithkeeper." This hour-long film was advertised in a catalogue published and circulated by Films for the Humanities and Sciences (P.O. Box 253, Princeton, NJ 08543-2053). A description of the film in the catalogue says that "the extent to which Native American philosophies have affected the dominant American culture is explored."

# 1996

## *Books, Scholarly, and Specialty Journals*

**1996.001.** _____. "Iroquois Confederacy Formed Basis for U.S. Constitution." *Indian Life Magazine* 17:1 (March/April, 1996), p. 9.

> This brief piece, adapted from the *Cherokee Advocate*, published in Tahlequah, Oklahoma, notes that the Cherokees "belong to the Iroquois language family," and that "the Iroquois were extensively studied and praised by Benjamin Franklin and Thomas Jefferson. They often referred to it as the basis for the United States Constitution." *Indian Life* is published in Winnipeg, Manitoba.

**1996.002.** _____. "The Iroquois Confederacy." *Peace Research Review* 14:1 (January, 1996), pp. 100-104.

> This description of the Iroquois Confederacy is numbered "XVIII," indicating that it is part of a worldwide survey of federal systems of government. This piece says that even the most conservative estimates of the Iroquois League's origins (about 1500 A.D.) make it older than the Swiss cantons, and "in a modern study of federations the Iroquois Confederacy is particularly relevant because of its influence on the Founding Fathers of the American constitution." (p. 100) "When looking at the number of countries that have constitutions based on the American model, the influence of the Iroquois Confederacy can be felt." (p. 104) Much of the factual support for this survey piece is drawn from *Forgotten Founders* (1982, 1987), *Exemplar of Liberty* (1991), and Donald Grinde's *The Iroquois and the*

*Founding of the American Nation* (1977).

**1996.003.** Abrams, Terry C. [Review, Lyons, *Exiled in the Land of the Free* (1992)] *Red Ink*, July 6, 1996.
[http://www.smu.edu/~twalker/review_e.htm]

> Abrams says that *Exiled in the Land of the Free* "offers proof that Native Americans, especially the Iroquois Confederacy, have had a profound influence on the formation of the U.S. Constitution." *Red Ink* is a Native American student magazine produced at the University of Arizona.

**1996.004.** Bordewich, Fergus M. *Killing the White Man's Indian: Reinventing Native Americans at the End of the Twentieth Century.* New York: Doubleday, 1996.

> Bordewich, a roving editor for the *Readers' Digest,* provides a short take on the influence issue on page 298 of this combination travel narrative and polemic: "Indians are now commonly taught to believe that American democracy is based on the Iroquois Confederation, a curious notion that relies on a handful of rhetorical remarks by Benjamin Franklin." Elsewhere in this book, the author writes that the Lakota claim to the Black Hills is "recent and contrived," and that environmental metaphors in Chief Sea'thl's speech were "invented." Bordewich also calls Oren Lyons an advocate of "Indian superiority." On "influence," Bordewich lists as bibliographic sources Johansen, *Forgotten Founders* (1982,1987), Weatherford, *Indian Givers* (1988), and Oren Lyons, *et al., Exiled in the Land of the Free* (1992).

**1996.005.** Bork, Robert H. *Slouching Toward Gomorrah: Modern Liberalism and American Decline.* San Francisco: ReganBooks/ HarperCollins, 1996.

> One of the many ways in which modern liberalism is destroying U. S. culture, according to neoconservative lawyer Bork, is "curriculum changes to accommodate multiculturalist pressures." (p. 306). "We have already seen this in feminist and Afrocentric studies," writes Bork, "but it is everywhere." (p. 306) Sounding so much like earlier assertions of this theme that he borders on plagiarism of George Will, and others, as many as seven years earlier, Bork hauls out the notion that "In New York State it is official educational doctrine that the

United States Constitution was heavily influenced by the political arrangements of the Iroquois Confederacy." (p. 306) Bork strains to find a word that expresses the type of "political arrangement" maintained by the Iroquois. Bork also ignores the fact that a lively debate has grown up over the issue, as he pontificates: "The official promulgation of this idea was not due to any research that disclosed its truth," but because "the Iroquois had an intensive lobbying campaign." Bork rests his case on assertions that agree with him by John Leo, in his polemic *Two Steps Ahead of the Thought Police* (New York: Simon & Schuster, 1994, p. 307) and Arthur Schlesinger, Jr.'s *Disuniting of America* (1992).

**1996.006.** Champagne, Duane. "A Multidimensional Theory of Colonialism: The Native North American Experience." *Journal of American Studies of Turkey* 3 (1996): 3-14.
[http://www.bilkent.edu.tr/~jast/Number3/Champagne.html]

Champagne comments: "Cultural exchange in the colonial situation was carried by interpersonal interaction with missionaries, traders, colonial officials, slaves, and other colonists. To varying degrees both the indigenous peoples and colonizers got to know each other's language, culture, economy, political norms, and social relations. Ideas, words, economic techniques, forms of dress, and many other cultural and normative items were selectively appropriated by each group. In recent years, some cultural theorists have focused on the effects on subject peoples of cultural domination. But, it is also critical to understand the extent to which the colonized internalized selected aspects of the colonizer's culture. The cultural knowledge gained from the colonizer by the colonized was used to build resistance to colonization and/or promote acceptance and participation in the colonizer's new order." *Exemplar of Liberty* is referenced.

**1996.007.** Charest, Paul. [*Review: Native American Political Systems and the Evolution of Democracy: An Annotated Bibliography*] *Anthropologie et Sociétés* 20:3(1996), p. 159. [in French]

**1996.008.** Churchill, Ward. *From A Native Son: Selected Essays on Indigenism, 1985-1995.* Boston: South End Press, 1996.

On page 275, Churchill argues that the influence of the Iroquois on the formation of American governance (as well as the genesis of Marxism) is largely missing in the study of political science, citing Grinde and Johansen, *Exemplar of Liberty* (1991). On page 343, Churchill notes that "the influence of the Haudenosaunee [Iroquois] on the formation of the democratic ideals expressed by the founding fathers."

**1996.009.** Dittemore, M.R. [Review, Johansen, *Native American Political Systems and the Evolution of Democracy: An Annotated Bibliography*] *Choice* 34(November, 1996), p. 432.

> "...a timely issue that is part of a larger debate concerning how history is written. Recommended for all libraries with interests in American history studies, Native Americans, communication, or journalism." Dittemore is with Smithsonian Institution Libraries.

**1996.010.** Foster, Michael K. [Review, Hanni Woodbury, *Concerning the League: The Iroquois League Tradition as Dictated in Onondaga by John Arthur Gibson*, comp. Hanni Woodbury, Reg Henry, and Harry Webster on the basis of A. A. Goldenweiser's manuscript. Algonquian and Iroquoian Linguistics, Memoir No. 9. Winnipeg, Manitoba: University of Manitoba Press, 1992.] *International Journal of American Linguistics* 62:1(1996), pp. 117-120.

> Near the end of his review, Foster says that "Woodbury has done a remarkable job of reconstituting a text of central importance to the Iroquois and students of the Iroquois." He adds, in a footnote: "To say nothing of those engaged in the present debate over the influence of the Great Law on the United States Constitution." Foster cites Grinde and Johansen, *Exemplar of Liberty* (1991) and Tooker (1988).

**1996.011.** Francis, Lee. *Native Time: A Historical Time Line of Native America.* New York: St. Martin's Press, 1996.

> This reference book contains, on p. 117, description and quotation of Canassatego's speech at the Lancaster Treaty Council (1744) advising the colonists to form a union on the Iroquois model. On pp. 328-329, the book's "Prologue, 1994 and beyond" quotes extensively from a speech given by President Bill Clinton at a tribal summit in Washington, D.C., May 2, 1994: "So much of what we are today comes from who you have been for a long time. Long before others came to these shores

there were powerful and sophisticated cultures and societies here -- yours. Because of your ancestors, democracy existed here long before the Constitution was drafted and ratified." The evening before he gave this speech, Clinton had been given a copy of *Exemplar of Liberty* (1991) by Lummi Jewell (Praying Wolf) James as part of a gift-giving ceremony at the White House.

**1996.012.** Grinde, Donald A., Jr. "Place and Kinship: A Native American's Identity Before and After Words," in Becky Thompson and Sangeeta Tyagi, eds. *Names That We Call Home: Autobiography of Racial Identity*. New York: Routledge, 1996.

Grinde discusses his work on the "influence" issue after Iroquois elders asked him to study the subject in the early 1970s.

**1996.013.** Grinde, Donald A., Jr. and Bruce E. Johansen. "Sauce for the Goose: Demand and Definitions for 'Proof' Regarding the Iroquois and Democracy." *William & Mary Quarterly*. Third Ser. LIII, No. 3(Summer, 1996), pp. 621-636.

After editors of *The William & Mary Quarterly* accepted for publication two articles opposed to the "influence" thesis [see Levy (1996) and Payne (1996), below], they invited Grinde and Johansen to rebut in a forum titled "The 'Iroquois Influence' Thesis -- Con and Pro. " The result is a detailed discussion of standards of proof in the debate in one of North America's most venerable historical journals.

**1996.014.** Halbritter, Ray. "Indian Economic Futures: Governance and Taxation." *Vital Speeches of the Day*, December 15, 1996 (Vol. 63, No. 5, p. 153).

Halbritter, nation representative of the Oneida Indian Nation (in New York State), is speaking at a forum on the economic future of Native American nations sponsored by the American Indian Program of Cornell University, November 13, 1996. Halbritter surveys the growth of gambling and other business enterprises on Oneida territory as well as elsewhere in Indian Country, finding that federal and state governments have not heretofore sought to tax Native American nations because there was little to gain. Today, for the first time, says Halbritter, "a handful of Indian nations are enjoying a small measure of economic prosperity." Halbritter also provides a brief history of the Oneida Nation and the Iroquois Confederacy, during which he says: "Many historians maintain that the Confederacy provided a democratic model that the framers of the United States Constitution later used in crafting the federal government." He cites Lyons, ed., *Exiled in the Land of the Free* (1992).

**1996.015.**  Herrick, James W.  "Iroquois League," in *Academic American Encyclopedia.*  Danbury, Conn.: Grolier, 1996, Vol. 10, pp. 222-223.

At the end of this brief entry on the Iroquois League, on p. 223, Herrick writes: "Some historians claim that the highly democratic political organization of the Iroquois League may have served as a model for the compilers of the United States Constitution."

**1996.016.**  Iverson, Peter.  [Review of Hauptman, *Tribes and Tribulations*] *Ethnohistory* 43:4(Fall, 1996), pp. 729-731.

Iverson notes that Hauptman "proceeds to add his voice to what appears to be a never-ending procession of individuals who wish to comment on the Iroquois contributions, or lack thereof, to the writing of the U.S. Constitution." Iverson writes that Hauptman uses James Wilson to suggest "that those who have supported the idea of significant Iroquois influence have overstated the case...[which he says is] 'speculative at best.'"

**1996.017.**  Jennings, Francis.  *Benjamin Franklin: Politician.*  New York: W.W. Norton, 1996.

On page 86, Jennings quotes Franklin's 1751 letter to his printing partner James Parker: "It would be a very strange thing if six Nations of ignorant Savages should be capable of forming a Scheme for such an Union, and be able to execute it in such a Manner, as that it has subsisted ages, and appears indissoluble, and yet that a like Union should be impracticable for Ten or a Dozen English Colonies." Jennings, who reads Franklin without nuance, writes that "some Iroquois propagandists" have "seized upon" this quote to "claim Franklin as an endorser of their traditional tribal league." Jennings, who does not name the "Iroquois propagandists," writes that: "How this contempt for 'ignorant Savages' can be twisted into praise for them is beyond my comprehension."

**1996.018.** Johansen, Bruce E. "Debating the Origins of Democracy: Overview of an Annotated Bibliography." *American Indian Culture & Research Journal*, Vol. 20, No. 2 (Summer, 1996), pp. 155-172.

> Summary of Johansen, *Native American Political Systems and the Evolution of Democracy: An Annotated Bibliography*.

**1996.019.** Johansen, Bruce E. *Native American Political Systems and the Evolution of Democracy: An Annotated Bibliography.* Westport, Conn.: Greenwood Press, 1996.

> Roughly 460 sources on the debate to late 1995.

**1996.020.** La Vere, David. [Review: *The Native Americans*, 1994] *Journal of American History* 83:3(December, 1996), pp. 1113-1114.

> This review of Turner Entertainment's *The Native Americans* notes in passing that the TV series includes "contributions made by Indians, such as the high status of Indian women and the influence of the Iroquois Confederacy in the creation of the U.S. Constitution."

**1996.021.** Levy, Philip A. "Exemplars of Taking Liberties: The Iroquois Influence Thesis and the Problem of Evidence." *William & Mary Q.*, Third Ser., LIII, No. 3(Summer, 1996), pp. 588-604.

> Levy and Samuel B. Payne (1996, below) critique the work of Grinde and Johansen, who offer a rebuttal in this forum, "The 'Iroquois Influence' Thesis -- Con and Pro." *See also*, Grinde and Johansen, 1996, above.

**1996.022.** Manus, Peter M. "The Owl, the Indian, the Feminist, and the Brother: Environmentalism Encounters the Social Justice Movements." *Boston College Environmental Affairs Law Review* 23 (Winter, 1996), p. 249.

> In footnote 112, Manus, associate professor at the New England School of Law, writes: "It is interesting to note that a number of scholars have observed that the philosophers and politicians credited with having developed the concept of United States democracy...drew heavily on their study of how the Indian nations of Eastern North America governed themselves." *Exiled in the Land of the Free* (1992) is cited.

**1996.023.** Markoff, John. *Waves of Democracy: Social Movements and Political Change.* Thousand Oaks, Calif.: Pine Forge Press, 1996.

> In this study of ideological change in democratic thought, Markoff writes, on page 39, "In the centuries that followed the voyages of Columbus, European discussion of political institutions sometimes showed significant awareness of the non-European world....It is certain...that some were quite fascinated by, say, the Indians of North America, as were Thomas Jefferson and Benjamin Franklin, for the latter of whom the world's outstanding model of decentralized federalism was the Iroquois." *Forgotten Founders* (1982, 1987) is cited.

**1996.024.** Mihesuah, Devon A. *American Indians: Stereotypes and Realities.* Atlanta, Ga.: Clarity Publishers, 1996.

> This book takes up various stereotypes attributed to Native Americans, one of which is "Indians had nothing to contribute to Europeans or to the growth of America." The author writes, on page 55, that "The American Founding Fathers (such as Thomas Jefferson, James Madison, and Benjamin Franklin)...were influenced not only by European writers such as Locke, Rousseau, and Montesquieu, as well as ideas found in the Magna Carta and the Greek and Roman empires, but also by the powerful, well-organized Haudenosaunee (Iroquois) *Kaianerekowa* (Great Law of Peace)."

**1996.025.** Newhouse, David R. and Ian D. Chapman. "Organizational Transformation: A Case Study of Two Aboriginal Organizations." *Human Relations* 49:7(July, 1996), p. 995.

> This article is based on the authors' perception of how two Canadian Native groups tried to change their organizational structures from those imposed by the Canadian government to "those based on traditional aboriginal values more typically found in collectivist societies." In this context, the authors note that "Historically, many tribes had elaborate traditional forms of government, some so sophisticated that they were one source of the U.S. constitution." Grinde and Johansen, *Exemplar of Liberty* (1991) is cited.

**1996.026.** Nies, Judith. *Native American History.* New York: Ballantine, 1996.

On pp. 80-81, this book recounts in some detail (with some phrasing from *Exemplar of Liberty*) Benjamin Franklin's observations of the Iroquois League in operation during the early 1750s, and his use of the Iroquois as a model in the Albany Plan of 1754, as he "began to contemplate a political instrument of unity for the colonies based on some of the ideas of the Iroquois." On pp. 184-185, Nies develops the "influence" idea in greater depth, quoting Oren Lyons.

**1996.027.** Norgren, Jill. *The Cherokee Cases: The Confrontation of Law and Politics.* New York: McGraw-Hill, 1996.

Page 28: "[American Indian law]...was, however, thoroughly grounded in the Europeans' belief in the preeminence of their values even though some founders of the republic were familiar with the Great Law of the Iroquois, and might have incorporated [it] into the developing Anglo-American legal system. This legal system, some argue, provided a legal facade for the denial of Indian rights." Norgren cites Renee Jacobs, "The Iroquois Great Law and the United States Constitution: How the Founding Fathers Ignored the Clan Mothers" (1991).

**1996.028.** Parillo, Vincent N. *Diversity in America.* Thousand Oaks, Calif.: Pine Forge Press, 1996.

This survey of ethnic diversity in North American history briefly discusses Iroquois consensus building on p. 31, noting that some historians "have identified this primitive democracy form as a prototype for such provisions of the United States Constitution as reconciliation of differing Senate-House legislation, impeachment, and expansion of new partners." Parillo cites Weatherford, *Indian Givers* (1988).

**1996.029.** Payne, Samuel B., Jr. "The Iroquois League, the Articles of Confederation, and the Constitution." *William & Mary Q.,* Third Ser., LIII, No. 3(Summer, 1996), pp. 606-621.

Payne and Philip A. Levy (1996, above) critique the work of Grinde and Johansen, who offer a rebuttal in this forum, "The 'Iroquois Influence' Thesis -- Con and Pro." See also, Grinde and Johansen (1996, above).

**1996.030.** Pratt, Scott L. "The Influence of the Iroquois on Early American Philosophy." *Transactions of the Charles S. Peirce Society* 32:2(Spring, 1996), pp. 275-314.

> Pratt examines "possible connections between what we might call a Native American philosophical perspective and what we recognize as early American philosophy," finding that no published studies make this connection. Pratt studies the writings of Cadwallader Colden, Benjamin Franklin, Alexis de Toqueville, John Adams, Thomas Jefferson, and others. He finds that philosophical discussion of Native America was copious in the writings of the period, centering often on the Iroquois Confederacy. Along the way, Pratt considers Iroquois influence "in the development of the form of the United States government." (p. 278). Scott cites *Forgotten Founders* (1982, 1987) and mistakenly attributes to it an assertion that "U.S. political structures were all but copies of the Iroquois confederate structure." This essay also cites Barreiro (1992) and Venables (1992) on the "influence" issue.

**1996.031.** Royal Commission on Aboriginal Peoples [Canada]. *Report of the Royal Commission on Aboriginal Peoples.* Ottawa, Canada: Government of Canada. 5 vols. 1996.

> Iroquois influence on democracy is raised twice in this five-volume work: Volume 1 ("Looking Forward, Looking Back,") pp. 53, 91, and Volume 2 ("Reconstructing the Relationship,") pp. 243, 403. Citations include: Grinde, *Iroquois and the Founding of the American Nation* (1977), Johansen, *Forgotten Founders* (1982, 1987), Tooker, "Constitution and the Iroquois League" (1988), and Grinde and Johansen, *Exemplar of Liberty* (1991).

**1996.032.** Spicer, Michael W. [Review of Fox and Miller, *Postmodern Public Administration*, 1995] *American Review of Public Administration* 26:2(June, 1996), p. 251.

> In reviewing Fox and Miller's book, Spicer disagrees with their assertion that "The [U.S.] Constitution was a plagiarized version of the Iroquois government structure."

**1996.033.** Starna, William A. and George R. Hamell. "History and the Burden of Proof: The Case of the Iroquois Influence on the U.S. Constitution." *New York History*, October, 1996, pp. 427-452.

Starna, long a strident critic of the "influence" idea, and Hamell, of the New York State Museum, take issue with Grinde and Johansen's work, especially concerning Canassatego and the 1744 treaty conference at Lancaster, Pa. Starna and Hamell ransack footnotes, providing the most intense scrutiny of Grinde and Johansen's work to date. They find a handful of factual errors that they admit are minor. This piece concludes, however, with a roundhouse condemnation of Grinde and Johansen's scholarship, and a declaration that they have, in Elisabeth Tooker's words, perpetuated a monumental hoax.

**1996.034.** Straub, Deborah Gillan, ed. *Voices of Multicultural America: Notable Speeches Delivered by African, Asian, Hispanic, and Native Americans.* Detroit: Gale Research, 1996.

This volume contains the nomination speech of Ada Deer for the office of Commissioner of Indian Affairs, before the Senate Indian Affairs Committee, July 15, 1993. The speech develops "the major contributions American Indians made to democracy and the federal government system." Deer describes Native American, particularly Iroquois, influences on Franklin, Jefferson, and Paine, with wording that sounds as if it comes from Johansen, *Forgotten Founders.*

**1996.035.** Stubben, Jerry. [Review of Hauptman, *Tribes and Tribulations* (1995)]. *American Indian Culture and Research Journal* 20:1(1996), pp. 253-256.

Stubben praises Hauptman's collection of nine essays as well written and documented, but "Hauptman's use of the psychological profile of James Wilson to rebut Donald Grinde's and Bruce Johansen's argument that the Iroquois and other Native American nations influenced the founding fathers in their development of democracy in America is less than convincing." By concentrating on Wilson, "a minor player in Iroquois/colonial relations," writes Stubben, "Hauptman overlooks the the influence of Native American political thought on major players such as Franklin, Jefferson, and Rutledge."

**1996.036.** Thompson, William N. *Native American Issues: A Reference Handbook.* Santa Barbara, Calif.: ABC-CLIO/Contemporary World Issues Series, 1996.

In an overview of Native American political sovereignty (on p. 5), Thompson notes that "the federal union of the five Iroquois nations and the Tuscarora not only preceded the union formulated by the founding fathers of the U.S. Constitution, but it was a model closely studied by the likes of Thomas Jefferson, Benjamin Franklin, and other founding fathers of the United States..." On page 90, on an historical timeline, Thompson writes that Franklin "followed the structure of the Iroquois Confederation" in his Albany Plan of 1754. Thompson cites Felix Cohen (1942), Johansen, *Forgotten Founders* (1982), and Jose Barreiro (1992).

**1996.037.** Wagner, Sally Roesch. *The Untold Story of the Iroquois Influence on Early Feminists: Essays by Sally Roesch Wagner.* Aberdeen, S.D.: Sky Carrier Press, 1996.

This 50-page booklet contains Wagner's four earlier-published articles tracing intellectual debts of nineteenth century feminists such as Matilda Joslyn Gage and Elizabeth Cady Stanton to their experiences with Iroquois women. The four articles are republished from *On the Issues* (1995), *Northeast Indian Quarterly* (1992), *Akwesasne Notes* (1989), and *Changing Men* (1989).

**1996.038.** Washburn, Wilcomb E. and Bruce G. Trigger, "Native Peoples in Euro-American Historiography," in Trigger and Washburn, eds. *The Cambridge History of the Native Peoples of the Americas.* Cambridge, England: Cambridge University Press, 1996.

On page 113, Washburn and Trigger condemn the "influence" idea with no factual argument, but no shortage of invective, tying its advocates to those who assert that Europeans invented scalping. They cast the argument as "the idea...that the American Constitution was consciously patterned on the government of the Iroquois Confederacy," which, they say, "found [its] champions among a Euro-American audience (which included historians) until their fragile supports were undermined by other historians and anthropologists." The main players in this intellectual rumble are listed in a footnote: Grinde, Johansen, Lyons, and Tooker.

**1996.039.** Wearne, Phillip. *Return of the Indian: Conquest and Revival in the Americas.* Philadelphia: Temple University Press, 1996.

In this survey of Native American history and modern-day revivals, Wearne on page 38 quotes Benjamin Franklin's advice to his printing partner James Parker in 1751 that the colonies should unite on an Iroquois model. He also notes Canassatego's advice to the colonists along similar lines (printed by Franklin) in 1744, as well as the symbols of the eagle and the bundle of arrows on the United States Great Seal. On p. 196, the reference to Canassatego is repeated in a timeline.

**1996.040.** Zimmerman, Larry J. *Native North America: Living Wisdom.* Boston: Little, Brown, 1996.

This survey of Native American cultures briefly describes the Iroquois League, and then adds, on p. 41: "They [The Iroquois] also set an example to the leaders of the United States through their political acumen."

## *Newspapers, Magazines, and Newsletters*

**1996.041.** _____. "Family: Entertaining Options...Children's Books." Cleveland *Plain Dealer*, September 14, 1996, p. 3-E.

This piece contains a review of Trudy Griffin-Pierce's *Encyclopedia of Native America* (New York: Viking, 1995), which is being marketed for children 10 years of age and older. The review says that in the encyclopedia, "The reader learns that the Six Nations' League of the Iroquois influenced Benjamin Franklin's conception of the American Constitution."

**1996.042.** _____. "Leon Shenandoah." The Glasgow [Scotland] *Herald*, July 24, 1996, p. 16.

This obituary of Leon Shenandoah, who died July 22, notes that he was Tadadaho (speaker) of the Iroquois Confederacy, an office that can be "traced back in an unbroken line to Hiawatha, who helped [with Deganawidah, the Peacemaker] to bring the 'Great Peace' that formed the confederacy sometime between the years 900 and 1350. Many historians believe that America's founding fathers based the United States Constitution and form of government on the Iroquois system." The same piece also appeared in The Milwaukee *Journal-Sentinel* on the same date, p. 5.

**1996.043.** _____. "Test Your Knowledge of Women's Accomplishments in History." Idaho Falls *Post-Register*, March 13, 1996, p. B-3.

> Question 14 of this quiz on women's history asks: "In the 1600s, the constitution of the Iroquois Confederacy guaranteed women the sole power to regulate war and peace. True or false?" A similar test appeared March 6, 1996 in the St. Petersburg (Florida) *Times*, on page 5-D. Some of the questions are different. The question on the Iroquois Confederacy is the same, but as question 8 on this list. the *Times* piece is under the name of Jennifer L. Stevensonse.

**1996.044.** _____. "What's On-line." Houston *Chronicle* (Business Section), December 29, 1996, p. 6.

> This survey of on-line information resources includes a description of resources on the University of Oklahoma Law Center's U.S. Historical Documents home page at http://www.law.uoknor.edu/ushist.html. The database is said to include, among many other things, the text of the Magna Carta and President Clinton's latest state of the union address, as well as the inaugural addresses of each U.S. president. This website also contains, according to this article, "...the first constitution written on North American soil -- that of the Native American Iroquois nation."

**1996.045.** _____. "Book Notes." Omaha *World-Herald* (Entertainment), September 8, 1996.

> Brief mention of Johansen's work on *Debating Democracy* (1998) and *Native American Political Systems and the Evolution of Democracy: An Annotated Bibliography* (1996).

**1996.046.** _____. [Review of Johansen, *Native American Political Systems...*, 1996] *Book News* [Portland, Oregon], September 1, 1996.

> This review says that the annotated bibliography on the "influence" debate "cites and substantially annotates books, newspaper articles, book reviews, academic articles, films, speeches, documentaries and even some stage plays that take a position one way or another on whether Native American, and specifically Iroquois...influenced modern democracy."

**1996.047.** _____. "Considering Indigenous Equity." *Links: Women's Studies Program.* [University of Illinois at Urbana/Champaign] February, 1996, p. 11.

> Brief announcement that Sally Roesch Wagner's article "Is Equality Indigenous?" is available on the Reading Rack at Women's Studies House.

**1996.048.** Ackerman, Todd. "Radio Host Recuperates After Being Hit By Driver." Houston *Chronicle*, March 9, 1996, p. A-29.

> University of Houston Professor John Lienhard, host of the National Public Radio show "The Engines of Our Ingenuity," was recovering in hospital after his legs were broken by a motorist who hit him deliberately. Lienhard, 65, was walking his two dogs near his home when the unidentified motorist swerved off the adjoining street and hit him. Police are speculating that Lienhard was the victim of a gang initiation rite. This article concludes: "Its [Lienhard's show] 3 1/2 minute essays have considered everything from manhole covers to the invention of chewing gum to the debt the U.S. Constitution owes to the Iroquois nation's political system."
>
> Lienhard's commentary "The Iroquois and U.S. Government," was number 709 (undated) in his NPR series, and is said by Lienhard to be the most-requested printed version of any of his commentaries. The text is available on the World-wide Web at http://www.uh.edu/admin/engines/epi709.htm. "Today," begins Lienhard, "we find a surprising blueprint for our government." Lienhard outlines Canassatego's advice that the colonists form a league like that of the Iroquois in 1744, and Benjamin Franklin's reaction to this advice and other events in the Albany Plan of 1754, observing several similarities between United States and Iroquois political customs and law. Lienhard concludes: "In the end Canassatego and the Iroquois tipped the scale in shaping our way of life. And we can be very glad they did." Lienhard cites Jack Weatherford's *Indian Givers* (1988).

**1996.049.** Atkinson, Nancy. "Our Debt to Native Americans." [Letter to the Editor] Minneapolis *Star-Tribune*, April 13, 1996, p. 22-A.

> Atkinson agrees with an April 3 commentary by Katherine Kersten that American history curricula need "study of diverse

cultural heritages that came together to create our country."
She finds, however, that Kersten omitted Native Americans
from her analysis: "...[S]he failed to mention that the
flowering of democracy came not so much from the ideals of the
ancient Greeks and Romans, but from the ideals of a nation that
the founders witnessed right here on this continent: the League
of the Iroquois." Atkinson points out that the Iroquois had a
federal system, that women had a part in it, and that "caucus"
is an Algonquian word.

Sally Roesch Wagner provided a second (unpublished) reaction
to the same column from Sanford Berman, head cataloguer of
the Hennepin County Library, Minnetonka, Minnesota. Berman
wrote, in part: "Before extolling White, Western civilization
as the sole source of American democracy, Katherine Kersten
(April 3) might have done a subject search in Hennepin County
Library's on-line catalogue under "Democracy -- United States:
Native American Influences." Berman writes that several
books have been written on the subject that Kersten could have
read at local libraries, including *Exemplar of Liberty* (1991),
*Exiled in the Land of the Free* (1992), and *Indian Roots of
American Democracy* (1992).

This column brought another unpublished letter from Susan M.
Breedlove, a teacher at Patrick Henry High School in
Minneapolis. She wrote to Kersten, in part: "Your article does
not address the concept of democracy in the U. S. in a holistic
manner. You have left out a major factor...how the American
Indian helped shape democracy." She advises that Kersten
read *Forgotten Founders* (1982, 1987), providing a citation for
that book and several others, along with a letter on the same
subject that Breedlove wrote to Hillary Rodham Clinton.

**1996.050.** Carpenter, Paul. "The Directive Avoids Focus on
Ourselves." Allentown [Pennsylvania] *Morning Call*, September
29, 1996, p. B-2.

In an editorial column, Paul Carpenter of the *Morning Call*
discusses a Pennsylvania state resolution requiring that
students in that state be taught about "organized attempts to
eliminate certain ethnic groups." The Jewish Holocaust, the
Irish potato famine, and slavery are specifically mentioned,
but Carpenter finds that nothing is said about American
Indians. Phil Armstrong, a history teacher at Allentown's

Whitehall High School, is quoted as saying that the state directive does not even mention the Wounded Knee massacre of 1890. Carpenter, visiting Armstrong's classes, was asked to tell the students something they didn't know about American Indians. "I told them that the U.S. Constitution is based largely on the governmental system of a particular Indian group. Which group? That stumped them....The class had focussed on Plains Indians, and I'm originally from New York state, where we learned a lot about the Iroquois."

**1996.051.** Clinton, Bill. "Presidential Proclamation on American Indian Heritage Month." U.S. Newswire, Oct. 30, 1996, in LEXIS.

President Clinton may have read Winona Laduke's speech accepting the vice-presidential nomination of the Green Party on August 31, 1996. He may also have read Louise Erdrich's piece in the Washington *Post* June 23, 1996 (below). Both invoked the idea that Clinton used in a proclamation observing Native American Heritage Month, as he said: "It was the Iroquois who taught that in every deliberation we should consider the impact of our decisions on the next seven generations." Clinton's proclamation also observed that "Throughout our history, American Indian and Alaska Native peoples have been part of the American character."

**1996.052.** Colson, John. "A Quick Dip in Some Native Americana." The Aspen [Colorado] *Times*, July 6 & 7, 1996. [http://www.aspenonline.com/aspenonline/directory/times/dir/96/Jul/week1/hit.html]

Colson, a columnist for the Aspen *Times*, comments: "I spent some time absorbing a small dose of Native American wisdom this week, and if nothing else, I was fascinated. For five hours in the middle of the busiest day of the busiest week of the summer, as far as my job goes, I sat on a stump at the Aspen Center for Environmental Studies and listened to representatives of the Utes, the Hopis and the Iroquois talk about their cultures, their prophesies, their fears....My day at ACES was mostly consumed by an amusing, instructive and eloquent talk by one Thomas Porter, a retired clan leader from the Mohawk nation back East, which is part of the six-nation Iroquois Confederacy. He related the legend of the Iroquois "Peace Messiah" who a millennium ago was born to a virgin and grew up to unite an entire region of warring tribes and establish a multinational regime that has endured for a thousand years. He described the basics of their system of government, which some believe was a central inspiration for the Founding Fathers as they fashioned the U.S. Constitution."

**1996.053.** Erdrich, Louise. "Read Their Lips! Three Novel Ideas for a Clinton Speech." Washington *Post* [Outlook], June 23, 1996, p. C-1.

The editors of the Washington *Post* Outlook section asked three novelists to write their version of President Bill Clinton's acceptance speech for renomination at the Democratic National Convention. One of the three was Erdrich, who included the following in her version of the speech: "Brothers and sisters, let us bend eagerly to the task before us and not allow the partisanship of the campaign to deter us from our essential work. The men and women of the League of the Iroquois, our earliest political organization, from which Benjamin Franklin drew inspiration for our form of government, based decisions not on short-term political gain, but considered what the effect of each act would have upon the seventh generation."

**1996.054.** Fedr, Don. "Victim Nation Meets Public Ed." Boston *Herald*, October 14, 1996, p. 25.

In an editorial column, Fedr observes that the previous week New York Gov. George Pataki signed legislation mandating that the Irish potato famine be taught in New York Public Schools. Fedr argues that education is becoming political turf for "victimologists" to the point that "New York also instructs its students that the U.S. Constitution was heavily influenced by the politics of the Iroquois, a politically correct fantasy for which the state's Indians successfully lobbied." Fedr is in error; the Iroquois curriculum on which this statement is based has not been implemented. Fedr, who identifies himself as Jewish, wonders how he got through school with his self-esteem intact, without the benefit of being told of the uniqueness of his people's suffering. He is concerned that "multiculturalism is dividing us into warring clans, hypersensitive, hyphenated Americans." Besides, he concludes, "Europe just happened to originate democracy, capitalism, the rule of law, science, advanced technology, and other aspects of civilization whose flowering on these shores has made America the place where everyone else on earth wants to be."

**1996.055.** Henry, Elisabeth. "This Holiday in Native American Terms." Tannnersville [New York] *Mountain Eagle*, November 27, 1996.

> This article on the Native American roots of Thanksgiving quotes John Kahionhes Fadden on the influence of women in Iroquois society, and adds: "Our Founding Fathers borrowed from the governments of the Six Nations (Iroquois) in forming our own enlightened Constitution."

**1996.056.** Hoshikawa, Jun. "Native Nations." *International GEO* 3:9 [In Japanese] September, 1996, pp. 48-51.

> This survey of American Indian history, published in Japan, includes material linking the Iroquois great law to the development of democracy in the United States, from *Exemplar of Liberty* (1991). Author Hoshikawa also postulates that Iroquois law had an influence on the development of other social ideas and movements, including communism, feminism, and environmentalism.

**1996.057.** Jacobs, Alex. "Tribes Victims Again." *Indian Time* 14:1 (January 12, 1996), p. 6.

> In a letter to the editor of *Indian Time*, a newspaper serving the Akwesasne Mohawk reservation, Jacobs protests proposals to tax goods and services on Indian lands. He asserts: "What about your missing $100 million in uncollected [state] taxes? We are still missing millions due us by treaty....We are missing land-claims settlements." Jacobs says that "The Iroquois were inspirations for the Constitution, the concept of separation of powers and democracy itself." The irony, argues Jacobs, is that "these 'concepts' do not seem to apply to us."

**1996.058.** Johansen, Bruce E. "A Political Correctness Horror Story," *Nuestro Mundo* (Omaha), March, 1996, p. 2.

> Part one of a two-part series of columns on the debate regarding the Iroquois and the evolution of democracy.

**1996.059.** Johansen. "More on Iroquois Law and American History," *Nuestro Mundo* (Omaha), April, 1996, p. 2.

Part two of a two-part series of columns on the debate regarding the Iroquois and the evolution of democracy.

**1996.060.** McCabe, Marsha. "True Root of Democracy." *Sunday Standard-Times* [Bedford, Mass.], November 24. 1996, n.p.

McCabe, a regular *Standard-Times* columnist, uses Jerry Mander's *In the Absence of the Sacred* to reflect on mainstream American debts to the Iroquois political system in a Thanksgiving Day context. She examines the Albany Plan of 1754 and writes that, "eventually, these Indian concepts made their way into the Articles of Confederation and the Constitution."

**1996.061.** Pelphrey, Jonathan. "Johansen's Expertise, Book Spark Interest, Debate." University of Nebraska at Omaha *Gateway*, August 30, 1996, pp. 1, 2.

Summary of Johansen's work on *Debating Democracy* (1998) and *Native American Political Systsems and the Evolution of Democracy: An Annotated Bibliography* (1996).

**1996.062** Phillips, Steve. "'Multicultural' Must Include Whites." San Francisco *Examiner*, May 20, 1996, p. A-19.

Phillips, president of the San Francisco Board of Education, asserts that "While there exists a growing acknowledgement that education should reflect the cultural diversity of the student population, we rarely discuss the implications of such changes for whites." He notes that 50 percent of San Francisco's population (but only 13 percent of its public school students) are white. Phillips writes that "A narrow Eurocentric curriculum not only alienates, it does a significant disservice to white students....A student who understands the annexation of the Southwest, Reconstruction...and the Iroquois influence on the U.S. Constitution will have a much better grasp of history than someone who studies only George Washington, Abraham Lincoln, and Andrew Carnegie."

**1996.063.** Ryan, Grace. "The Voice of Indigenous Women: Today and Yesterday." *HONOR Digest* (Milwaukee) January/February, 1996, p. 5.

The newsletter of HONOR (Honor Our Neighbors' Origins and Rights), a Native American support group, describes Iroquois influence on nineteenth-century feminists Elizabeth Cady Stanton, Lucretia Mott, and Matilda Joslyn Gage, as researched by Sally Roesch Wagner. Parallels are drawn to the Fourth World Conference on Women in Beijing.

**1996.064.** Sloan-Spice, Shannon. "Wouldn't It Be Nice If..." *HONOR Digest,* March/April, 1996, p. 10.

This newsletter of HONOR (Honor Our Neighbors' Origins and Rights) carries an account of a paper that was dropped off at its office in Milwaukee, Wisconsin by Shannon Sloan-Spice, "student activist and HONOR member." The paper, titled "The Great Law of Peace and the American Constitution," describes the role of women in the Iroquois Confederacy, and advocates more equal treatment of women in mainstream American society.

**1996.065.** Strait, Douglas E. "Iroquois League Served as Basis for Constitution." Columbus (Ohio) *Dispatch,* March 26, 1996, p. 6-A.

In a letter to the editor, Strait, of Columbus, takes issue with J. Matthew Todd's remarks in a recent letter to the editor that the United States was "founded on Christian principles" and that the U.S. Constitution was "based on biblical principles." Strait writes that the founders took their inspiration from many sources, including the Iroquois League. He mentions the Albany Plan of Union, but dates it at 1744, not 1754. The Albany Plan was based on the Iroquois system, Strait asserts. "Franklin's proposal languished for several decades until, at Philadelphia, the delegates turned to its provisions and based the final Constitution on much of the Iroquois ideals."

**1996.066.** Thomas, Jane Resh. "Children's Books: Kids Can Avoid a Sketchy Sense of the Past...Native American Encyclopedia Makes History Vivid." Minneapolis *Star-Tribune,* February 11, 1996, p. 15-F.

This is a review of Trudy Griffin-Pierce's *Encyclopedia of Native America* (Viking, 1995), for ages 10 and up, in which "The reader learns that the Six Nations League of the Iroquois influenced Benjamin Franklin's conception of the Constitution."

**1996.067.** Washburn, Wilcomb E. "Clear-eyed View of Indian Life." Washington *Times*, February 18, 1996, p. B-7.

> This review of Fergus M. Bordewich's *Killing the White Man's Indian: Reinventing Native Americans at the End of the Twentieth Century* (1995) praises the author for following in the footsteps of James Clifton's *Invented Indian* in debunking what Washburn takes to be erroneous beliefs about American Indians. The book, written by a roving staff reporter for *Reader's Digest*, states, according to Washburn, that the Lakota claim to the Black Hills is "recent and contrived," and that environmental metaphors in Chief Sea'thl's speech were "invented." Washburn also reports that Bordewich "dismisses the notion that the Iroquois Confederation provided American colonial statesmen with the basic ideas underlying the American Constitution." Bordewich also "ridicules Bill Moyers for seeming to swallow whole the charismatic Onondaga Oren Lyon's [*sic*] assertion [on his Public Broadcasting series, Bill Moyers' Journal] that the Iroquois had foreseen most of the political and ecological problems confronting the white man." Washburn directs the Smithsonian American studies program.

**1996.068.** Worthington, Bob. "Questions About Local Water Supply." [Letter to the editor] Tampa *Tribune*, October 12, 1996, p. 17.

> "Watching our county planners and managers address our consumable water problem concerns me about our future," Worthington writes to the editor of the Tampa *Tribune*. "Once again, it seems that nearsighted greed has led us to ignore the wisdom that Ben Franklin gained from the Iroquois League (American Indian Democracy) and...used for the basis of our Constitution: a successful democracy must have at its foundation the premise that individuals do not act for individual gain alone, but...for the good of the whole union...meaning the need to respect physical limits of Mother Earth."

## Internet Web Sites

**1996.069.** [http://thebeadsite.com/frontier5. html] In a detailed discussion of wampum's indigenous roots and adaptions by English and Dutch colonists in the New World, observes that while Native Americans did not use wampum as money, it was adopted early as legal tender in most or all of the European colonies in North America. Wampum, which was used in ceremonies and as part of diplomatic protocol by many native people (particularly the Iroquois) was adopted because of a scarcity of European legal tender in America; in 1679, guests in New Amsterdam hotels paid their bills in wampum. Part of this piece observes that "The rules of the Iroquois Confederacy were admired by Benjamin Franklin and others and...many of its provisions were used as a basis for the Constitution of the United States of America." Electronic text supplied by John Kahionhes Fadden, received July 22, 1996.

**1996.070.** The Cleveland Freenet, aa300, Cybercasting Services Division, National Public Telecomputing Network, supplied by John Kahionhes Fadden, received August 2, 1996. Gerald Murphy wrote a 10,000-word piece on the "Iroquois Constitution," noting that he "found sufficient data and evidence to convince me that the Iroquois most certainly did have a considerable influence on the drafting of our own Constitution." Murphy's search was begun by a reference to the idea in Charles Mee's *The Genius of the People* (1987).

**1996.071.** "Anthro-1 Archives, a discussion group mainly for academic anthropologists, contains several discussions of the "influence" issue with headings such as "The Iroquois and the Constitution" and "The Iroquois and Radical Feminists." Commentary ranges widely, and includes support from Prof. Joseph O'Neal, St. Edwards University (Austin, TX), and skepticism by Prof. Thomas L. Kavanagh, Indiana University, citing several works by Grinde, Johansen, and Wagner. See, for example, [http://www.anatomy.su.oz.au/danny/anthropology/anthro-1/archive/july1996/0357.html.]

**1996.072.** David Schneider and Louis Furmanski. "The International Personality of Indigenous Peoples: An Account from North America." A paper prepared for delivery at the 1996 Annual Meeting of the American Political Science Association, San Francisco, August 29-September 1, 1996. [http://www.geocities.com/CapitolHill/8366/indian.html] "Historically," the authors write, "members of the international community have been very reluctant to recognize indigenous peoples as equal players in the international arena. The indigenous inhabitants of North America were generally considered to be nothing but conquered ethnic minorities. The power and influence that these indigenous peoples once exercised was quickly forgotten once European settlements came to dominate the economic and political arena....The Iroquois Confederacy have consistently held that they have never ceased to be the same Confederacy that stood equal to

France, Britain, and the United States in the seventeenth and eighteenth centuries....It is a concept intrinsic to Iroquois identity, tradition, and history."

**1996.073.** San Diego State University. Instructional Technology Center (Acquisitions). Description of episodes, CBS "500 Nations." 1996. [http://www.rohan.sdsu.edu/dept/its/support/resources/acqs9697. html] Episode: "Cauldron of War." Description: "In 1776, 13 colonies united in a war to gain independence from England. But the nation that resulted from that conflict was not the first democracy in America. That distinction belonged to the Haudenosaunee (Iroquois) nation, independent states whose democratic framework was an inspiration to Benjamin Franklin when he met Iroquois leaders in 1754. Europe fights for control of American resources, turning Indian homelands into a cauldron of war....A decade after Pontiac's war, the colonies assert their right to form a democracy in a revolution that, ironically, splinters the democratic Iroquois nation."

## Other Items

**1996.074.** The Six Nations Indian Museum, Onchiota, New York, describes the Iroquois system of government and ways in which it shaped United States institutions in the text accompanying a painting created by John Kahionhes Fadden, June, 1996.

**1996.075.** Prepared testimony, Henry Cagey, Chairman, the Lummi Indian Nation, before the Senate Indian Affairs Committee, September 24, 1996. Cagey builds an historical case for the constitutional roots of Indian treaties, reminding legislators along the way that House and Senate resolutions passed in the late 1980s "proclaimed the intent 'to acknowledge the contribution of the Iroquois Confederacy of nations to the development of the United States Constitution, and to reaffirm the continuing government-to-government relationship between the Indian tribe and the United States established in the Constitution.'"

**1996.076.** Proclamation, State of New York, signed by Gov. George E. Pataki, Sept. 12, 1996. The proclamation observes that "Native Americans are the original inhabitants of the lands that now constitute New York State. New Yorkers are the beneficiaries of the rich cultural heritage of the Iroquian and Algonquian peoples who continue to live in this great state." The statement notes Native American contributions to settlers' foods and forms of shelter, as well as governmental institutions: "The early settlers dealt with Indian nations on a government-to-government basis. The Iroquois Confederacy

(Haudenosaunee) developed principles of freedom of speech and separation of powers in government, which principles form the foundation of our government today." The proclamation sets aside the fourth Saturday of September as "Native American Day" in New York State. A copy of the proclamation was received from John Kahionhes Fadden via Irving Powless, of the Iroquois Grand Council, January 30, 1997.

# 1995

## Books, Scholarly, and Specialty Journals

**1995.001.** _____. *Indian America: A Traveler's Companion.* Santa Fe: John Muir Publications, 1995.

> In this travel guide, the section on the Iroquois, on page 168, acknowledges that "Our U.S. Constitution was modeled after the organization of this unit."

**1995.002.** _____. "Iroquois Confederacy." *Gale Encyclopedia of Multicultural America:* Volume 2. Detroit: Gale Research, 1995.

> Page 761: "Although disputed by some, there is significant evidence that the Iroquois Confederacy served as a model or inspiration for the U.S. Constitution. Benjamin Franklin and Thomas Paine were well acquainted with the League....The Iroquois form of government...included elements equivalent to the modern political tools of initiative, referendum, and recall." This entry cites the published proceedings of the 1987 Cornell conference on the subject (See Barreiro, 1988, 1992).

**1995.003.** Bruchac, Joseph, ed. *New Voices From the Longhouse.* Greenfield, N.Y.: Greenfield Press, 1995.

> This collection of poetry, prose stories, and history from contemporary Haudenosaunee (Iroquois) includes a reference (on p. 217) to the examination of the Iroquois role in the development of democracy in Barreiro (1988, 1992).

**1995.004.** Cassidy, James J., Jr. *Through Indian Eyes: The Untold Story of Native American Peoples.* Pleasantville, N.Y.: Readers

---

Digest Association, 1995.

> This large, coffee-table format book uses Native American perspectives as its defining format. On page 148, under the heading "A Model for Union?" the text says that United States democracy had several antecedents, including the Iroquois League. A brief summary then follows, from Canassatego's advice that the colonists unify on an Iroquois model (1744), to the Albany Plan of Union (1754), and parts of the U.S. Constitution that resemble it. The borrowing of the eagle as a national symbol also is noted, along with the symbolism of the arrows.

**1995.005.** Clinton, Robert N. "Symposium Rules of the Game: Sovereignty and the Native American Nation: the Dormant Indian Commerce Clause." *Connecticut Law Review* 27(Summer, 1995), p. 1055.

> Clinton, who is Wiley B. Rutledge Professor of Law at the University of Iowa College of Law (as well as associate justice of the Cheyenne River Sioux Tribal Court), surveys the Iroquois role in British and French colonial history. This 47,000-word article contains a detailed treatment of the Albany Congress of 1754, which contains a footnote (#68) about the debate over Franklin's debt to the Iroquois. Clinton cites Grinde and Johansen, *Exemplar of Liberty* (1991), Johansen, *Forgotten Founders* (1982, 1987) and Grinde, *Iroquois and the Founding of the American Nation* (1977) as well as shorter works on both sides of the debate.

**1995.006.** Conaway, James. "Cultures at War." *Civilization: the Magazine of the Library of Congress*, March/April, 1995, pp. 28-33.

> This cover story in *Civilization* is an extended review of "500 Nations," a television series on American Indian history hosted by Kevin Costner and broadcast nationally. Conaway finds the series visually rich, but "often preachy and vague." He complains that few white people get cut much slack in "500 Nations," but that one of them is Benjamin Franklin, who was impressed by the Iroquois practice of democracy and federalism, and left the Iroquois imprint, along with many others, on his drafts of the Articles of Confederation.

**1995.007.** Deloria, Vine, Jr. "The Western Forum: The Struggle for Authority." *Journal of the West* 34:3(July, 1995), pp. 3-4.

> Deloria is responding to concerns expressed by Francis Paul Prucha in the January, 1995 issue of *Journal of the West* (below) that a "gap" is emerging and widening between "solid historical accounts and the pseudohistorical or mythical accounts adopted by many Indians and their white advocates." Instead, writes Deloria, "The truth is that the discipline of historical writing is beginning to move from its centuries-long simplistic doctrinal interpretation of history as a *good white man-bad Indian* scenario." Deloria believes that "The real issue underlying Prucha's complaint is based on authority and status. His examples of revisionist, and presumably inaccurate, history and his descriptive language illustrate what I would call the pitiful complaint and anguish of the old orthodoxy." Deloria then outlines the idea that the Iroquois helped shape democratic thought, and says that such ideas "were not refuted" by Prucha, "They were simply attacked." Deloria continues: "The point that the old school apparently misses is that one of the critical issues faced by the constitutional generation was the distribution of sovereign political powers between the new federal government and the colonies." The Six Nations had long since resolved this problem, he believes. "...[I]t seems absurd to continue to maintain that the founding fathers choose the course they did out of sheer genius." Deloria scoffs, as well, as the belief that "Andrew Jackson was the best friend Indians ever had," a reference to earlier writings by Prucha. He concludes: "Scholars should not worry that pristine historical study is undermined by new ideas or efforts to correct ancient wrongs. *That is the nature of continuing scholarship.*" [emphasis in original]

**1995.008.** Doxtator, Deborah. "Testimony Before the U.S. House of Representatives, Ways & Means Committee," May 1, 1996. (In LEXIS)

> Doxtator, chairwoman of the Oneida Tribe of Indians of Wisconsin, began her testimony on tax reform before the House Ways and Means Committee: "We are a member nation of the Iroquois Confederacy from which this American government learned the concept of a government of, by, and for the people. We are proud that our model of governmental checks and balances, upper and lower houses, and separation of powers became the foundation for the America."

**1995.009.** Foster, Michael K. [Review of Woodbury, Hanni, *Concerning the League...*] *American Anthropologist* 97:3(1995), pp. 582-583.

> Foster, who works with the Canadian Museum of Civilization, writes in his review of Woodbury's rendition of John Arthur Gibson's account of the Great Law of Peace that given "events of the colonial period...down to the present-day heated debate over the historical influences of the Great Law of Peace on the American constitution...it is surprising that no adequate version of the [Iroquois] League Tradition existed in print before *Concerning the League.*"

**1995.010.** Fox, Charles J. and Hugh T. Miller. *Postmodern Public Administration: Toward Discourse.* Thousand Hills, Calif.: Sage Publications, 1995.

> On page 67, discussing "The Foundations of Constitutionalism," Fox and Miller write: "At an intellectual level, anything that attempts to pass itself off, in postmodern conditions, as canonical (like the founding of a constitution or some distant social contract) will be debunked, deconstructed, and dismissed." Fox and Miller believe that, "The radical nominalism of postmodernism is singularly hostile to claims of universality....If constitutionalists assert one version of the founding, the Iroquois can provide a different version of how the founding came to be. (That is to say, what white Americans take to be the founding was nothing but a plagiarized version of the Iroquois governance structure)."

**1995.011.** Gitlin, Todd. *The Twilight of Common Dreams: Why America is Wracked by Culture Wars.* New York: Henry Holt, 1995.

> On pp. 201-202, Gitlin brings Iroquois precedents into a discussion of history as seen from various points of view, as expressed in the debate over national standards for the teaching of history. "Pure relativism is brittle....The partisans of fundamental group difference rank their own stories higher than others....To the challengers' eyes [what is being challenged is unclear] the Iroquois Confederacy *was* the model for the federal system of government enshrined in the Constitution -- although the evidence that the Iroquois system decisively influenced the writing of the Constitution is mixed." In an endnote, Gitlin cites Donald Grinde's chapter in Lyons,

*Exiled in the Land of the Free* (1992), calling the account "sometimes exaggerated."

**1995.012.** Grinde,. Donald A. Jr. "The Iroquois and the Development of American Government." *Historical Reflections* 21:2 (Spring, 1995), pp. 301-318.

> This is a survey of the "influence" case, drawn largely from *Exemplar of Liberty* [1991].

**1995.013.** Jackson, Sandra and José Solis. *Beyond Comfort Zones in Multiculturalism: Confronting the Politics of Privilege.* Westport, Conn.: Bergin & Garvey, 1995.

> In this anthology's first chapter, ("White Studies, the Intellectual Imperialism of U.S. Higher Education," pp. 17-36) Ward Churchill writes, "In political science, readers are invited -- no, defied -- to locate the course acknowledging, as John Adams, Benjamin Franklin, and others among the U.S. 'Founding Fathers' did, that the form of the American Republic and the framing of its Constitution were heavily influenced by the pre-existing model of the Haudenosaunee..." (p. 20). Churchill cites Grinde and Johansen, *Exemplar of Liberty*. A second reference to the "influence" issue appears in chapter 6, "Academic Apartheid: American Indians Studies and 'Multiculturalism.'" by Marie Annette Jaimes-Guerrero, pp. 89- 111. Page 101: "In yet another systemic and therefore covert act of racism, there is the absence or downplaying of the democratic contributions of native nations in the historicism of U.S. nationalism, as in the case of the Iroquois Confederacy in the East, which influenced the American system of government," This chapter also references *Exemplar of Liberty*, and earlier works by Grinde and Johansen.

**1995.014.** Jaimes-Guerrero, M. A. "Shifting Paradigms for an Anti-colonialist Discourse: Afterword." *Historical Reflections* 21:2(Spring, 1995), pp. 385-391.

> The author surveys ways in which "the contemporary United States continues to subjugate the traditional, indigenous peoples within its borders" (p. 386). On page 387, the "influence" issue is raised: "Eurocentric scholarship consistently discounts and trivializes indigenous accomplishments, perpetuating stereotypes of 'primitive' peoples and cultures who failed to

attain European 'standards' in agriculture, engineering, pharmacology, metallurgy, and religion. In a similar fashion, there is a reluctance to acknowledge the contribution of indigenous democracy, particularly that of the Iroquois Confederacy, to American governance. Only recently has the Native scholar Donald Grinde[,] working with Bruce Johansen [,] successfully brought this matter to public attention." *Exemplar of Liberty* (1991), Grinde's *Iroquois and the Founding of the American Nation* (1977) and Johansen's *Forgotten Founders* (1982, 1987) are cited in a footnote.

**1995.015.** Kickingbird, Kirke. "What's Past is Prologue: The Status and Contemporary Relevance of American Indian Treaties." *St. Thomas Law Review* 7 (Summer, 1995), p. 603.

Kickingbird is director of the Native American Legal Resource Center and assistant professor at the Oklahoma City University School of Law. He is also a Kiowa. He surveys the role of Indian treaties in United States law, writing that, "The concept of an Indian confederation of governments was well-known to the colonial governments along the Atlantic Coast. The most powerful example was the Iroquois Confederacy which Benjamin Franklin suggested as a model for colonial alliance at the Albany Conference in 1754." Kickingbird then quotes Canassatego at Lancaster in 1744 advising colonial representatives to form a union on an Iroquois model.

**1995.016.** Lewis, David Rich. [Review, Lyons, *et al.*, *Exiled in the Land of the Free. Journal of the West* 34:3(July, 1995), pp. 121-122.

Lewis finds "little that is new" in *Exiled*. The idea that the Iroquois had an impact on the development of American democracy, he writes, "will remain a 'glass half-empty, glass half-full' argument based on rather weak evidence."

**1995.017.** Lewis, David Rich. "The Native Americans." [Video Review] *American Historical Review* 100:4 (1995), p. 1200.

This review of the Ted Turner series "The Native Americans" mentions that in the first segment, "The Broken Chain," "John Mohawk (Seneca) broaches the subject of Iroquois antecedents to American republicanism."

**1995.018.** McDougald, Dana. [Review of videotape, "America's Great Indian Nations."] *School Library Journal*, August, 1995, p. 63.

> The Iroquois are one of six Native American nations examined in this hour-long video treatment for grades seven and later. McDougald says in this review that "Their great law of peace attracted the attention of American colonists who were forging their own new country. It is believed that much of our Constitution is based upon that of the Iroquois nation."

**1995.019.** Means, Russell. *Where White Men Fear to Tread.* New York: St. Martin's, 1995.

> On page 370 of this autobiography, Means discusses Iroquois notions of sovereignty: "They have endured for more than eight centuries....The U.S. Constitution was patterned after the code of their Confederacy."

**1995.020.** Merriam, Louise A. and James W. Oberly. *United States History: A Bibliography of the New Writings on American History.* Manchester, U.K.: Manchester University Press, 1995.

> This bibliography lists *Exemplar of Liberty* (1991) in its section on "The Constitution and its Interpretation."

**1995.021.** Miller, Lee, ed. *From the Heart: Voices of the American Indian.* New York: Knopf, 1995.

> On page 100, this collection of quotations from Native American authors and orators quotes Canassatego's advice at the Lancaster Treaty Council that the colonists should unite in a way similar to that of the Iroquois Confederation.

**1995.022.** Nies, Judith. [Review, Lyons, *et al.*, *Exiled in the Land of the Free*, 1992]. *Harvard Review* 9 (Fall, 1995), n.p.

> Nies agrees with Rodney Smolla's review in the New York *Times* (1992) that this book's great strength is that "it forcefully injects many of the most vexing questions about our constitutional past into our present discourse." "The case for the Iroquois influence on the shape of the U.S. Constitution is one part of the story," concludes Nies, "The use of the Constitution to deprive Indians of the[ir] lands and their rights...is another."

**1995.023.** Pommersheim, Frank. *Braid of Feathers: American Indian Law and Contemporary Tribal Life.* Berkeley: University of California Press, 1995.

> On page 122, Pommersheim excerpts from President Bill Clinton's speech to tribal leaders May 2, 1994 which mentions Native American democratic traditions that existed before the Constitution was proposed. For a text, see "Francis, Lee," above (p. 46). Pommersheim is quoting from the *B.I.A. Indian News Week-in-Review,* May 13, 1994, p. 1.

**1995.024.** Powless, Robert E. "Iroquois Indians." *The World Book Encyclopedia:* Volume 10. Chicago: World Book, Inc., 1995.

> In a brief entry on the Iroquois (p. 455), Powless notes that "the confederation of states that became the United States of America may have been patterned after the League."

**1995.025.** Prucha, Francis Paul. "Western Forum: The Challenge of Indian History." *The Journal of the West* 34:1 (January, 1995), pp. 3-4.

> Prucha is worried that, "The gap is widening, I fear, between solid historical accounts and the pseudohistorical or mythical accounts adopted and proclaimed by many Indians and their white advocates....A good example, which has been around from [sic] some years, is the effort to make the Iroquois Confederacy the [sic] model for the United States Constitution and American democratic government. Books and articles advancing these claims have appeared, and they have been refuted by knowledgeable scholars...but the idea continues to get support....The differences between the Iroquois League and the Constitution are numerous and significant, but even granting similarities, to conclude that one was the model for the other is a simple *post hoc ergo propter hoc* fallacy." Vine Deloria, Jr.'s rebuttal to this opinion piece appeared in the July, 1995 issue of *Journal of the West* and is summarized above.

**1995.026.** Shenandoah, Joanne and Diane. *Education at the Ordway: Teacher Information Packet.* St. Paul, Minn.: Ordway Music Theatre, 1995.

> This is a lesson plan for a curriculum on Iroquois arts, society, and culture prepared by the Ordway Music Theatre, St. Paul,

Minn., the state of Minnesota's largest arts organization. The curriculum was developed in conjunction with a performance by Joanne and Diane Shenandoah, who are Oneida, at the Ordway. On page 9, the curriculum says that "The Great Law was studied by Benjamin Franklin. He was so impressed by the Iroquois form of government that...he called on the delegates to unite and emulate the Iroquois League." The curriculum cites Grinde, *Iroquois and the Founding of the American Nation* in its bibliography.

**1995.027.** Valencia-Weber, Gloria and Christine P. Zuni. "Symposium: Women's Rights as International Human Rights: Domestic Violence and Tribal Protection of Indigenous Women in the United States." *St. John's Law Review* 69(1995), p. 69.

Valencia-Weber, an associate professor in the University of New Mexico Law School, and Zuni, a visiting assistant professor at the same school, survey the treatment of women in indigenous cultures, including the Iroquois, and mention their role in shaping democracy, from *Exiled in the Land of the Free*.

**1995.028.** Venables, Robert W. *The Six Nations of New York: The 1892 United States Extra Census Bulletin.* Ithaca, N.Y.: Cornell University Press, 1995.

On page xi, part of his introduction to the 1892 "extra" census report, Venables mentions that Canassatego urged the colonists to unite on an Iroquois model at the 1744 Lancaster Treaty Council. Venables also mentions on the same page Franklin's 1751 letter to his printing partner James Parker. Even such a mild assertion of the "influence" idea is enough to earn Venables a rebuke from William A. Starna (1997, above).

**1995.029.** Wiessner, Siegfried. "American Indian Treaties and Modern International Law." *St. Thomas Law Review* 7(Summer, 1995), p. 567.

Wiessner, a profesor in the St. Thomas University School of Law, mentions Iroquois constitutional democracy, citing *Exiled in the Land of the Free* (1992) and Greg Schaaf, "From the Great Law of Peace to the Constitution of the United States: A Revision of America's Democratic Roots." *American Indian Law Review* 14 (1989), p. 323.

**1995.030.** Wilbur, C. Keith, M.D. *The Woodlands Indians.* Old Saybrook, Conn.: Globe Pequot Press, 1995.

This children's book contains a short description of the Iroquois Confederacy. According to Wilbur, "Many believe that the federal plan was modelled after this alliance." (p. 69)

**1995.031.** Wilson, Gail Hamlin, associate editor. *Dictionary of Indian Tribes of the Americas.* Newport Beach, Calif.: American Indian Publishing, 1995.

In Vol. II, p. 515 of this three-volume encyclopedia, the Iroquois Confederacy's founding and operations are described at length, concluding with this comment: "In 1754...Benjamin Franklin's Articles of Union [*sic*] are said to be based on the constitution of the Confederacy." This essay also describes Franklin's 1751 letter to his printing partner James Parker advising emulation of the "Six nations of ignorant savages...[whose] union...has subsisted ages."

**1995.032.** Weaver, Jace. "Original Simplicities and Present Complexities: Reinhold Niebuhr, Ethnocentricism, and the Myth of American Exceptionalism." *Journal of the American Academy of Religion* 63:2(Summer, 1995), pp. 231-247.

Weaver uses the works of Reinhold Niebuhr to critique the historical notion that the United States has a divine mission, or "manifest destiny" to spread its democratic traditions around the world. While Niebuhr himself criticized many aspects of the United States' imperialistic frame of mind, Weaver finds that he turned a rather blind eye to the histories of Native Americans, to the point of speculating "whether non-European peoples are capable of realizing that norm [of liberal democracy]." In a footnote on page 241, Weaver observes that Niebuhr ignored the fact that many Native American societies "had highly developed democratic institutions, some of which influenced the founders of the Republic." *Exemplar of Liberty* (1991) is referenced.

**1995.033.** Wood, Gordon S. "A Century of Writing Early American History, Then and Now Compared, or How Henry Adams Got It Wrong." *American Historical Review* 100:3 (June, 1995), pp. 678-696.

Gordon Wood concludes a wide-ranging survey of h istorical writing in the century since the founding of the *American Historical Review* (in 1895) by describing a late-twentieth century explosion in writing by and about American Indians. "But some anthropologists [*sic*] have gone further and have become determined to show that the Indians made significant contributions to America's political institutions, including the idea of federalism and the making of the Constitution....The squabble recently created by this tracing of supposed Indian influence on American democracy demonstrates that the desire to discover the roots of the United States still runs strong...and that early American history is as important and vital to people today as it was a hundred years ago." Johansen's exchange with Tooker in *Ethnohistory* (1990) is cited, with Lyons, *Exiled in the Land of the Free* (1992).

## *Newspaper and Magazine Articles*

**1995.034.** _____. "Cyberguide." *Netguide*, September 1, 1995, p. 107.

This is a summary of five "cybershops," one of which is called "The '60s Trading Post for the '90s." The article describes this cybershop as a counter-culture marketplace, "where the Freak Flag still flies." Along with merchandise, this web site (http://attitude.wwa.com) delivers text files such as "The Secrets of the Drug War," and "The Iroquois Nation Constitution and the Declaration of Independence."

**1995.035.** _____. "Science Instructor Wins Honor." Dallas *Morning News*, April 28, 1995, p. 2-K.

At the Plano Independent School District Elementary History Fair, in the Fifth Grade, Teresa Nocella of Christie School won first prize for her essay, "The Great Law of Peace vs. the U.S. Constitution."

**1995.036.** _____. "Oneida Film: Indian Money Tells the Tale." Minneapolis *Star-Tribune*, November 23, 1995, p. 30-A.

This piece announces that the Oneida nation (of Wisconsin) is planning to spend some of its casino profits to stake a feature film about Dolly Cobus (a.k.a. Polly Cooper), George

Washington's cook. The Oneidas supplied Washington's troops at Valley Forge with substantial amounts of food. The article says that "The Oneidas are right to want other Americans to recognize the distinctive Oneida experience -- that they were patriots during the Revolutionary War, [and] that the American Constitution may well incorporate ideas from the governing principles of the Iroquois Confederacy."

**1995.037.** Forrest, Elisabeth. "*Times* Slams Admiral Jeremy Boorda For Giving Credit Where Credit Is Due." Washington *Times*, November 8, 1995, p. A-18.

> In a letter to the editor, Forrest, who lives in Alexandria, Va., takes issue with an item in the *Times* editorial-page column "Inside the Beltway" (October 26, 1995), which criticized Admiral Jeremy Boorda, chief of naval operations, for sending a message to all commands "to honor the North American Indian's contribution to the form of government that we practice today." In "Inside the Beltway," an unnamed "senior veteran" is quoted as saying that this is an example of "the silly season of PC [politically correct] admirals," making him wonder "if I should laugh or cry." Forrest writes that Boorda said in his message that "concepts such as freedom of speech, the separation of powers in government, and the balance of power within government were patterned after the political systems of our Native American Indian nations." "Instead of mocking Adm. Boorda," writes Forrest, "this 'senior veteran' might remember that the great statesman Benjamin Franklin in 1754 wrote: 'It would be a strange thing if six nations of ignorant savages...'" The statement was actually made by Franklin in 1751, in a letter to his printing partner James Parker.

**1995.038.** George, Doug (Kanentiio). "Haudenosaunee Confederacy a Presence at the UN." *News From Indian Country*, Late September, 1995, p. 13.

> George comments: "For decades Native American leaders have been knocking at the doors of the United Nations, trying to get in so they can make their arguments for admission as sovereign states, an idea to which the United States is adamantly opposed. This is ironic because the Haudenosaunee were called to consult on the U.N.'s organization in the late 1940s, just as the Iroquois almost two centuries earlier were involved in the evolution of a federal structure of government in the United

States." See, for comparative purposes: Barbara Graymont. *Fighting Tuscarora: The Autobiography of Chief Clinton Rickard.* Syracuse, N.Y.: Syracuse University Press, 1973, below.

**1995.039.** Griffin-Pierce, Trudy. *Encyclopedia of Native America.* New York: Viking, 1995.

This children's encyclopedia, for ages 10 and up, notes that the Six Nations League of the Iroquois influenced Benjamin Franklin's conception of the Constitution. On page 32, Griffin-Pierce writes: "The League of the Iroquois was probably the most successful tribal alliance of any kind, and its principles greatly influenced the founding fathers of the United States. Benjamin Franklin...drew direct inspiration from the Iroquois League for the Albany Plan of Union." She continues, concluding this book's 10-page section on the Iroquois, "To European and American philosophers, as well as colonial leaders, the League represented the more just and humane forms of government that they had been seeking. The essence of the League...continues today to guide such organizations as the United Nations."

**1995.040.** Iglesias, David Claudio. "Video/Audio Reviews." *Native Peoples*, Fall/Winter, 1995, p. 84.

In a review of "A History of Native Americans" (Schlesinger Video Productions, 1994), a half-hour video for children, the reviewer says that "It covers the influence of the democratic Iroquois Confederacy on the nascent American political system."

**1995.041.** Johansen, Bruce E. "Sovereignty Summit." *Akwesasne Notes*, New Series 1:3 & 4 (Fall, 1995) pp. 78-80.

This description of the Constitutional Sovereignty Summit, held in Washington, D.C., June 22-24, 1995 includes quotations from two presentations by Iroquois faithkeeper Oren Lyons, who described Haudenosaunee governance "and ways in which it shaped the founding of the United States." (p. 79)

**1995.042.** Johansen. "Making History is Dirty Business." *Nuestro Mundo* (Omaha), February 1995, p. 2.

Commentary on some of the grittier intellectual disputes arising over the "influence" issue, particularly those extant between Don Grinde and James Axtell.

**1995.043.** Lewerenz, Dan. "Understanding Diversity Requires Education." Kansas State University *Collegian*, January 19, 1995. [http://www.spub.ksu.edu/ISSUES/v099B/SP/n081/opn-multicultural-lewerenz.html]

> In an opinion column, Lewerenz discusses what should be done with multicultural education, suggesting "that Canassatego stand with Madison among the founders of our nation [and] that the 'Mexican Cession' be referred to as the 'Mexican Conquest' (cession, indeed -- as if Mexico just called and said, 'We don't want this anymore, but we need a war to make it look official ... we'll just cede it to you')."

**1995.044.** McCaslin, John. "Inside the Beltway: the Great Pumpkin Speaks." Washington *Times*, October 26, 1995, p. A-5.

> Columnist McCaslin ridicules Chief of Naval Operations Admiral Jeremy Boorda for sending a directive to "all commands on land and sea" honoring Native American contributions to democracy in observance of Native American Heritage Month in November. "And you thought the great genius of our form of government was bequeathed by that race of kings across yonder ocean -- the Magna Carta, the common law, and all that? But it wasn't, according to eminent historian and political scientist Jeremy Boorda, who moonlights as chief of naval operations." Adm. Boorda encouraged all commands to "support programs and exhibits, publish items of interest in command bulletins, and promote maximum participation by military and civilian personnel." McCaslin quotes an unnamed "senior veteran" as calling this the silly season of politically correct admirals. The veteran is quoted as saying "I don't know whether to laugh or cry."

**1995.045.** Samuels, David. "Philanthropical Correctness: The Failure of American Foundations." *The New Republic*, September 18, 1995, p. 28.

> Samuels begins his piece with a description of a dinner held in San Francisco by the Council on Foundations to honor its retiring president, James Joseph, who left that position to serve as

ambassador to South Africa. Joseph, who developed these themes in more detail in a book published in 1995, said at the dinner, that his vision of charity combines "The civic habits of the Iroquois admired by Benjamin Franklin, the Afro-American passion for justice, [and] the neo-Confucian respect for benevolence and giving."

**1995.046.** Seton, Tony. "Candidating Game." San Francisco *Chronicle*, September 10, 1995, p. 6.

In a letter to the editor, Seton, of Mill Valley, California, writes that "The solution to all this gender bashing is not to have two political parties -- one male and one female -- as was suggested in a letter last week (Sept. 3)." Seton says that we should "take another lesson from our predecessors, the Iroquois, whose matriarchs chose their chiefs. Let's have one gender be the candidates and the other be the voters. And we could switch off roles every four years."

**1995.047.** Sharkey, Alix. "Inside Story: Indian Giver." *The Guardian* [England]. April 8, 1995, p. T-27.

Sharkey writes at length (5,880 words) on Lakota (Sioux) objections to the fact that Kevin Costner, whom they once adopted after his role in "Dances With Wolves," now plans to build a large casino and resort in the Lakotas' sacred Black Hills. Part of the piece quotes Webster Poor Bear, a Lakota, who, according to Sharkey's account, "grew up on the rez." "The Black Hills belong to the Lakota people," Poor Bear is quoted as saying. "There is absolutely no respect for the Hills, for Mother Earth, for our water, or the people it was taken from. It's all for monetary gain. They stole these lands from us, and made us captives on our own land and started leeching it for all it's worth. Stabbed us in the back. Wrote treaties and broke them. And the irony is that the U.S. Constitution is based on the 16-nation [sic] Iroquois Confederacy's Constitution."

**1995.048.** Wagner, Sally Roesch. "The Untold Iroquois Influence on Early Feminists." *Native American Press/Ojibwe News* [Bemidji, Minn.] October 22, 1995, pp. 1,5.

This is a reprint of Wagner's "Is Equality Indigenous," detailing Iroquois impact on feminists Lucretia Mott, Elizabeth Cady Stanton, and Matilda Joslyn Gage.

**1995.049.** Wandell, Jack. "Demonizing the Big Glass House." *Akwesasne Notes*, New Series 1:3 & 4 (Fall, 1995), pp. 118-120.

> The "Big Glass House" is the United Nations. Wandell describes right-wing attacks on it in the United States on the U.N.'s 50th anniversary. He begins his article: "Among the most notable legacies of the Haudenosaunee [Iroquois]...is the Charter of the...United Nations."

## Internet Web Sites

**1995.050.** Danny J. Blubaugh, "Deganawidah, Iroquois Prophet." June, 1995. Blubaugh briefly discusses the founding of the Iroquois League and its influence on Franklin and Jefferson, citing Johansen, *Forgotten Founders*. [http://www.bcca.org/srb/archive/950421-950720/1357.html]

**1995.051.** Sahtouris, Elisabet. *Earthdance: Living Systems in Evolution.* [http://www.ratical.com/LifeWeb/Erthdnce/chapter20.html]
In Chapter 20, "The Indigenous Way," Sahtouris writes: "The political science of the Haudenosaunee contributed much to the democratic Constitution of the United States, as the September 1987 *National Geographic* magazine and the later work of work of scholars such as Oren Lyons, Vine Deloria, Jerry Mander and Jack Weatherford have documented. The founding fathers of the U.S. were refugees from European tyrannies. It was among the Indians of the Haudenosaunee League, whom they called Iroquois, that they found democratic principles and practices at work....Unfortunately, while adopting the Indians' democratic forms, the founding fathers left out the equal role of women in governance, as well as the sacred contract with nature."

**1995.052.** *Exemplar of Liberty* and *Forgotten Founders* are cited in Glenn Morris. "For the Next Seven Generations: Indigenous Americans and Communalism." Fellowship for International Community, 1995. [http://www.well.com/user/cmty/fic/cdir/art/30morris.html] The author adds, in a footnote: "Unfortunately, the framers of the United States Constitution were not ready to integrate some of the more liberating elements of the Iroquois system, such as suffrage and political power for women, abolition of slavery, and periodic redistribution of societal wealth."

**1995.053.** Lyons, Oren. "Ethics, Spiritual Values and the Promotion of Environmentally Sustainable Development. Fifty Years of the World Bank, Over 50 Tribes Devastated." October 3, 1995.

[http://www.ratical.com/ratville/OrenLyons.html#development]
In an address to officials of the World Bank, Lyons described the
origins and structure of the Iroquois Confederacy, and its links to the
development of democracy. "A thousand years ago or more we the
Haudenosaunee, the Iroquois, were given the rules and processes of
democracy. The principles of this democracy are: Peace in mind and
community, Equity, which is justice for the people, and the power of the
good minds, which embodies good health and reason....This was a
seamless government that inspired Benjamin Franklin to say '...this is a
government that seems indissoluble.' It inspired the roots of western
democracy that we know today."

**1995.054.** "Native American Indians and the United States: A Model
for Cultural Change." [http://www.pafb.af.mil/DEOMI/natam95.
htm] Ms. Janet I. Jones, an Occupational Training Manager at Eglin Air
Force Base, Florida, served as a participant in the Topical Research
Intern Program at the Defense Equal Opportunity Management Institute
during February 1995. Her lengthy report on Native American models
for modern American culture appears to be part of an Air Force racial-
diversity program. The report identifies her as being of Native
American ancestry, but provides no tribal affiliation. Part of the report
says: "When our country's European forefathers crafted the
Constitution as the foundation for self-government, they modeled it
after the great Native American Indian nations that preceded them.
Because of the racist, sexist nature of the culture that accompanied
these democratic principles, however, they were not applied equally,
across all segments of the population." The report cites Weatherford's
*Indian Givers* (1988).

**1995.055.** "Natchat" [Native Chat] [http://bioc09.uthscsa.edu/
natnet/archive/nc/9509/0129.html] Re: Origin of Constitution Question
On September 18, 1995, lesele.rose-jarmin@m.cc.utah.edu (Lesele Rose-
Jarmin) wrote: "I am asking for information about the origin of the U.S.
Constitution. I heard that it was based largely on the...Iroquois
Confederacy. A high-school teacher at my school asked me to find out
about this because she would like to incorporate the "Invasion" as part
of her U.S. History class this year. A. Paul Antone, special projects
officer, Federal Archaeology Office, National Historic Sites
Directorate, Parks Canada, Department of Canadian Heritage replied:
"You should check the September, 1987 edition of the *National
Geographic* magazine (172:3). There is an article on page 340 titled
"James Madison: Architect of the Constitution" and on page 370 is
another entitled "From One Sovereign People to Another" about the
Iroquois Confederacy. See also: *Indian Roots of American Democracy*,
ed. José Barreiro, Akwe:kon Press, Cornell University, 1992. And yes,

[Antone added], the U.S. Constitution is based on the Iroquois Confederacy." He added: "The views and opinions expressed here are my own and they do not necessarily reflect those of the Department of Canadian Heritage or the Government of Canada."

**1995.056.** Giese, Paula. [Review of Evelyn Wolfson, *From Abenaki to Zuni: A Dictionary of Native American Tribes* (1995) in "Native American Books." [http://indy4.fdl.cc.mn.us/~isk/books/ya/ya337. html] Comments Giese: "This is one of the worst books (of its type, the very worst) I've ever seen." Among its many omissions, says Giese, this encyclopedia for young people omits "Iroquois League conceptual contributions to world order (or domestic formation of the U.S.), i.e. the idea of a multi-part governmental confederacy of equals. Agricultural, artistic, philosophic, and modern literary achievements -- gifts to the world -- are not mentioned for any tribe." [In Wolfson's defense, it may be noted that she developed the Iroquois influence on democracy at length in an earlier book for children specifically on the Iroquois. (Wolfson, 1992)]

## Other items

**1995.057.** Video Tape, "America's Great Indian Nations," Quester Home Video (Chicago, Ill.). This hour-long tape surveys the histories of the Iroquois, Seminole, Shawnee, Navajo, Cheyenne, and Lakota. Five times the script mentions the idea that the Iroquois political system helped shape democracy. The film briefly recounts the founding epic of the Iroquois and notes Benjamin Franklin's use of Iroquois concepts. Tape received from John Kahionhes Fadden (who contributed artwork to it) January 9, 1995.

**1995.058.** Kevin Costner's "500 Nations," an eight-hour documentary aired in four segments on CBS during the spring of 1995, contained references to Haudenosaunee government and Benjamin Franklin's use of its concepts. *TV Guide* (Vermont edition, supplied by John Kahionhes Fadden), provides a sketch of the show (on p. 71), which says that the segment to be aired May 27 shows "how the democratic Haudenosaunee inspired Ben Franklin to press for Colonial independence from England." The primary conduit of the "influence" idea in this case was Derek Milne, a doctoral student at the University of California -- Los Angeles who works with the American Indian Studies Center, publishers of *Exemplar of Liberty* (1991).

**1995.059.** The "influence" thesis figured into several presentations and roundtable discussions at the Tribal Sovereignty Summit, organized by the Lummi Nation Treaty Task Force at the behest of the National Congress of American Indians to define ways in which Native nations can exercise greater sovereignty, and to report to the President, Congress, and tribal leaders. The summit, held in Washington, D.C., June 22-24, included a detailed description of Iroquois governance by Oren Lyons; Grinde and Johansen also presented papers.

**1995.060.** Video Tape (30 minutes), "They Lied to You in School: Ray Fadden Speaks." White Buffalo Multimedia, Woodstock New York. No date on tape; circa 1995. On this tape Ray Fadden, founder of the Iroquois Six Nations Museum in Onchiota, New York, and Mohawk culture bearer, talks of Indian contributions to American society, including the role of Iroquois democratic traditions in shaping fundamental law in the United States.

**1995.061.** The Oneida Nation of Wisconsin used $40,000 in gambling profits to produce four public-service video spots (60, 30, 20, and 15 seconds each) describing "the Iroquois legacy of freedom and democracy," including influence on United States democratic institutions. The segments are titled: "Indians Then and Now: The Iroquois Confederacy." Director of the spots was Baba Cooper.

# 1994

## *Books and Scholarly Journals*

**1994.001.** Alschuler, Albert W. "A Brief History of the Criminal Jury in the United States." *University of Chicago Law Review* 61 (Summer, 1994), p. 867.

> As an aside in his study of the jury system, Alschuler writes that "A few Native American governments may have been more democratic in some respects, particularly in the extent to which they permitted women to participate in governmental affairs." Alschuler is Wilson-Dickinson professor at the University of Chicago Law School.

**1994.002.** Bennoune, Karima. "*As-Salumu Alaykum:* Humanitarian Law in Islamic Jurisprudence." *Michigan Journal of International Law* 15 (Winter, 1994), p. 605.

Bennoune describes Islamic contributions to international law, and decries attempts to trace world-wide standards for justice to any one (especially European) culture or geographic area. The author writes, in footnote 217, that "Such recognition of the multicultural roots of legal principles is occurring elsewhere in historical and legal studies. One such debate is that over the ...Iroquois, roots of the U.S. Constitution." This piece cites Stannard, *American Holocaust* (1992).

**1994.003.** Bernstein, Richard. *Dictatorship of Virtue: Multiculturalism and the Battle for America's Future.* New York: Alfred A. Knopf, 1994.

Bernstein, a long-time journalist with *Time* magazine and the New York *Times*, wanders wide-eyed through what he seems to regard as a brave new world of multicultural education. On his way, in Milwaukee, he visits an elementary school, Andersen Contemporary, which teaches Afrocentric and other multicultural curricula. Teachers at the school showed him a list of books that included *Exemplar of Liberty* (1991) and *Forgotten Founders* (1982, 1987) "demonstrating that the Algonquin [*sic*] system of government, the confederation of the five Algonquin tribes, was a model for the framers of the U.S. Constitution."

**1994.004.** Calloway, Colin. *The World Turned Upside Down: Indian Voices from Early America.* Boston: Bedford Books/St. Martin's Press, 1994.

On page 104, Calloway quotes Canassatego at the Lancaster Treaty Conference, July 4, 1744, in his advice to the colonists to unite on an Iroquois confederate model. He comments, rather simplistically, on page 100, that "Some people interpret Canassatego's words as evidence that, forty-five years later, the Founding Fathers based the United States Constitution on that of the Iroquois."

**1994.005.** Churchill, Ward. *Indians Are Us? Culture and Genocide in Native North America.* Monroe, Maine: Common Courage Press, 1994.

Page 149: "[Oren] Lyons is supported by a quote from Yamasee historian Donald Grinde on the influence of the Haudenosaunee on the formation of democratic ideas expressed by the Founding Fathers."

**1994.006.** Crawford, Neta C. "A Security Regime Among Democracies: Co-operation Among the Iroquois Nations." *International Organization*, Summer, 1994 (Vol. 48, No. 3) pp. 345-385.

> This article, published in the journal of the World Peace Foundation, Massachusetts Institute of Technology, outlines the formation and operation of the Iroquois Confederacy. Crawford compares the Iroquois League to the Concert of Europe, and says that it is an example of Immanuel Kant's idea of a system of "perpetual peace." The article conveys an erroneous impression that the Iroquois Confederacy ceased to exist in 1777, during the American Revolution. This article cites *Forgotten Founders* (1982, 1987).

**1994.007.** Harvey, Karen D. and Lisa D. Harjo. *Indian Country: A History of Native People in America.* Golden, Colo.: North American Press/Fulcrum, 1994.

> This teachers' guide for primary and intermediate-grade pupils mentions "influence" on page 48: "Many contemporary scholars credit the contribution that the Iroquois made to the current U.S. Constitution and Bill of Rights." On pp. 97-99, the Iroquois Confederacy is described, and, on p. 107, Benjamin Franklin's suggestion that the colonies emulate the Iroquois with a political union (in 1751) is mentioned on a timeline. *Forgotten Founders* (1982, 1987) is cited in the bibliography on p. 328.

**1994.008.** Leo, John. *Two Steps Ahead of the Thought Police.* New York: Simon & Schuster, 1994.

> On p. 307, Leo regurgitates the substance of at least three magazine columns in which he asserts that the "influence" idea is the invention of an Iroquois lobby in New York State.

**1994.009.** Snow, Dean R. *The Iroquois.* Oxford, U.K.: Blackwell, 1994.

> In his history of the Iroquois, Snow, a professor of anthropology at the State University of New York -- Albany, says that while "Franklin's aborted Albany Plan of Union probably drew some inspiration from the Iroquois," and "this idea is very popular with the general public and most politicians....There

is, however, little or no evidence that the framers of the Constitution sitting in Philadelphia drew much inspiration from the League." Snow argues, on p. 154, that "such claims muddle and denigrate the subtle and remarkable features of Iroquois government." However, concludes Snow, "the temptation to demonstrate that the United States Constitution was derived from a Native American form of government, for ephemeral political purposes, is too strong for some to resist." In a footnote (p. 238), Snow remarks that "I trust that, in the short term, but only in the short term, this paragraph [on p. 154, above] will be the most controversial offered in this book." He references Grinde and Johansen, *Exemplar of Liberty* (1991), Tooker's article in *Ethnohistory* (1988) and the Johansen-Tooker exchange in the same journal (1990). In the footnote Snow says that a "complete exposition" of the controversy would require a book, "if popular interest in it does not fade by the end of the century."

**1994.010.** Tiller, Veronica E. Velarde, ed. *Tiller's Guide to Indian Country: Economic Profiles of American Indian Reservations.* Albuquerque: Bow Arrow Publishing, 1994.

On page 477, under "Oneida Reservation," Tiller writes that "The Iroquois Confederacy authored the first federal constitution in North America, known as the *Gayaneshagowa* [Great Law of Peace]."

**1994.011.** Versluis, Arthur. *Native American Traditions.* Shaftsbury, Dorset, Great Britain: Element Publishers, 1994.

This pictorial survey mentions the Iroquois Confederacy briefly on page 14, "with [its] confederacy, a governmental model that, it has been suggested, served as one source of inspiration for the form of government adopted by the United States."

**1994.012.** Wells, Robert N., Jr. *Native American Resurgence and Revival: A Reader and Bibliography.* Metuchen, N.J.: Scarecrow Press, 1994.

In this general review of literature on Native American issues, Wells, on page 229, writes: "Another myth is contained in the suggestion that indigenous governmental forms were less advanced than their European counterparts. The enlightened republicanism established by the United States during the late

1700s -- usually considered a great advance over European norms -- was lifted directly from the still-functioning model of the Iroquois Confederacy (with considerable dilution of Iroquois egalitarianism)." Wells cites Donald Grinde's *Iroquois and the Founding of the American Nation* (1977).

**1994.013.** Williams, Robert A., Jr. "Linking Arms Together: Multicultural Constitutionalism in a North American Indigenous Vision of Law and Peace." *California Law Review* 82 (July, 1994), p. 981.

Williams describes in detail the origin and procedures of the Iroquois Confederacy and its Great Law of Peace, arguing, as his title indicates, that the Iroquois have an effective model for a multicultural society. He strives to "avoid overt engagement in the needlessly acrimonious debate about the degree of influence of Iroquois political ideas on the 'Founders' of the United States..." Williams, a professor of law at the University of Colorado, and a Lumbee Indian, lists sources on both sides, including Grinde (1977), Tooker (1988), Johansen (1982, 1987), Weatherford (1988), and Barreiro (1992).

## *Newspapers*

**1994.014.** Brown, Brian D. "Why We Need to Change the Way We Teach History." Washington *Times*, June 7, 1994, p. A-16.

In a letter to the editor, Brown, who identifies himself as "an African in America," takes issue with a May 24 op-ed piece by Samuel Francis titled "Giving Multiculturalism a Good, Swift Kick." "He needs to know," writes Brown, "that civilizations throughout the world had participatory forms of government. In addition, the model of our current government came from one of the groups that Francis belittles as 'charming savages.'"

**1994.015.** Holston, Noel. "Feelings Compete With Facts in TBS' 'Native Americans.'" Minneapolis *Star-Tribune*, October 10, 1994, p. 1-E.

This review of the Turner Broadcasting System's series "The Native Americans" finds it visually stunning and factually "impressionistic." "It conveys historical information about a variety of topics, from the impact of the Iroquois League on

Benjamin Franklin and Thomas Jefferson, to the Carlisle School."

**1994.016.** Kessler, Barbara. "How Aware Are You?" Dallas *Morning News*, April 25, 1994, p. 1-C.

Kessler offers a "multicultural awareness quiz" of 15 questions, one of which is: "Name the founders of the first representative government in what would become the United States." The answer is listed as "the Iroquois."

**1994.017.** Pine, Ed Kimmel. "Senator Hart Treated Unfairly." Pittsburgh *Post-Gazette*, July 17, 1994, p. NV-5.

Pine is making a case that the *Bible* was more important to the founding of the United States than the Constitution. He concludes: "The Iroquois Indians were certainly not the basis of our Constitution."

**1994.018.** Seigel, Suzie. "Setting the Record Straight on Facts of Indian History." Tampa *Tribune*, November 14, 1994, p. 1 [Baywatch Section].

This news story details the efforts of Donna M. Allen, a Cherokee, to collect "facts to combat the myths about American Indians." Her findings include the fact that the word "caucus" comes from Algonquian and that "The first person to suggest that the 13 Colonies form a union was the Iroquois chief Canassatego....Benjamin Franklin pitched the idea at the Albany Congress in 1754." Allen also asserts that the practice of giving each political unit an equal voice (as in the U.S. Senate) is patterned on Iroquois practice.

## *Other items*

**1994.019.** Film: "Kahnasatake [Oka]: 270 Years of Resistance," National Film Board of Canada, film maker Alanis Obomsawin. This two-hour film chronicles the crisis at Oka, Quebec, which flared into violence during the summer of 1990. The film, which won an award as Best Canadian Film at the Toronto Film Festival (1993), describes Iroquois history and governmental structure, including an assertion that the Iroquois system "influenced the adoption of a democratic charter in

North America." The film was shown on the Canadian Broadcasting System in early 1994.

**1994.020.** On April 29, 1994, the White House invited representatives of 545 Native tribes and nations to a conference to formulate a Clinton Indian Policy. This was the first time in the history of the United States that so many representatives had been invited to confer at once. In his remarks to the gathered Native leaders, Clinton referred to "our common heritage," including "sophisticated cultures...[including] democracy...long before the U.S. Constitution." The speech was broadcast live on C-SPAN.

**1994.021.** Eight images by John Kahionhes Fadden that were originally drawn for *Exemplar of Liberty* [1991], were used in a television documentary by Turner Broadcasting System (TBS), Atlanta, Georgia, which discussed the issue. The series of programs, "The Native Americans," was broadcast on TBS October 10, 11, and 13, 1994, and was sold afterwards on tape.

**1994.022.** "Trends in the News," Trends Research Institute [Rhinebeck, N. Y.] July 1, 1994. [Found in LEXIS]. The Trends Research Institute forecasts that, by the year 2005, American notions of patriotism will be refigured to include Native American traditions. "Laws also will reflect newly discovered elements of early Indian cultures. In fact, some of these elements, especially those of the Iroquois Confederacy, will experience a rebirth. Many Iroquois principles are said to have influenced the framers of the Constitution more than 200 years ago." This forecast was composed by Gerald Celente, director of the Trends Research Institute.

**1994.023.** Transcript, "Talk Back Live," Cable News Network, October 28, 1994. This talk show, which aired at 1 a.m. Eastern time, contained a segment in which Lynne Cheney, conservative director of the National Endowment for the Humanities under President George Bush, debated with Suzan Shown Harjo. The exchange covered a number of topics, one of which was assertion of Iroquois influence on the evolution of democracy. Harjo began the exchange, with reference to what sort of material should be taught in mainstream history books: "I think it's awfully important to learn about the very great framers of the United States Constitution, who were...the Iroquois people, the Natchez people, the Muskogie people [who influenced] Benjamin Franklin, [George] Morgan, and Jefferson, [who] found camaraderie with...nations confederated for peacetime purposes. They didn't find that working model in Europe; they found it here with the native confederacies." Cheney replied: "It's not at all clear that this...is historically accurate. This is a hotly debated point. I think that if [this] type of thing is to go into our textbooks, we certainly need to point out to students that it's a hotly debated point."

**1994.024.** Haudenosaunee Confederacy. "Onondaga Nation Banishes Three Law Violators." Press release: July 2, 1994. Nedrow, New York. [http://bioc09.uthscsa.edu/natnet/archive/nl/9407/0014.html]
This press release explains why the Council of Chiefs banished illegal smokeshop owners from the Onondaga Territory as an exercise of Iroquois sovereignty. "The United States recognized their independent national status in the Canandaigua Treaty of November 11, 1794, signed by President George Washington with the Onondaga and their six neighboring nations composing the famed Six Nation Iroquois Confederacy. Article 7 of this Treaty provides the process for dealing with this issue. The Confederacy and its customs and laws were cited as examples of sophisticated governmental practices by Benjamin Franklin during the early debates of the American Continental Congress."

# 1993

## *Books, Scholarly, and Specialty Journals*

**1993.001.** Banks, James A. *et al. The United States and its Neighbors.* New York: Macmillan/McGraw-Hill, 1993.

> On page 353, this fifth-grade textbook begins a two-page sidebar titled "Traditions...We the People," with artwork showing the Iroquois at a council meeting. The text says, in part: "The Iroquois League was a living example of what American leaders wanted to create when they set out to write the Constitution."

**1993.002.** Cantor, George. *A North American Traveler's Indian Guide: Landmarks.* Detroit: Gale Research, 1993.

> Under "New York -- Iroquois Indian Museum, Cobbleskill," on p. 210, Cantor notes that "Some scholars believe they [the Iroquois] also left behind [sic] a significant political heritage. The federal council of the Six Nations is regarded as one of the models the Founding Fathers used in drawing up a system for

the new American republic."

**1993.003.** Crawford, J. D. "Looking Again at Tribal Jurisdiction: 'Unwarranted Intrusions on Their Personal Liberty.'" *Marquette Law Review* 76 (Winter, 1993), p. 401.

> Crawford notes with some irony that while the U. S. House of Representatives Subcommittee on Constitutional Rights in 1967 held that tribal judges lacked experience, training, and familiarity with "the traditions and forms of the American legal system" history indicates that "the organization of the Iroquois Confederation influenced the Articles of Confederation."

**1993.004.** Hill, James F. "A Rationale for Native American Studies in a Secondary School Curriculum." Listed in ERIC [educational database], 1993.

> "This paper offers reasons why Native American culture and history should be included in the secondary school curriculum based on the fact that many ideas and products that are taken for granted today have Native American roots...[and] discusses the contributions to U.S. democratic society by Native American political structure[s], especially the Iroquois League." The paper then discuses various attributes of the Iroquois structure which also are found in the United States political system, including federalism and impeachment, while noting that the Founders did not adopt the equality of women found in the Iroquois system.

**1993.005.** Kotke, William H. *The Final Empire: the Collapse of Civilization and the Seed of the Future.* Portland, Ore.: Arrow Point Press, 1993.

> On page 255, in the midst of a detailed exposition on the Haudenosaunee Confederacy (much of it excerpted from *A Basic Call to Consciousness*) Kotke concludes: "This governing form [the Iroquois Confederacy] was the inspiration for the concepts of separation of powers and checks and balances found in the United States Constitution, concepts which have now spread throughout the world."

**1993.006.** Macklem, Patrick. "Distributing Sovereignty: Indian Nations and Equality of Peoples." *Stanford Law Review* 45 (May, 1993), p. 1311.

> Macklem is discussing ways in which Native American notions of liberty and sovereignty mesh with non-Indian traditions and beliefs. He notes that "...Many features of the American federal system were influenced by the structure of North American Indian confederacies." Macklem, who is an assistant professor of law at Toronto University, cites Grinde and Johansen, *Exemplar of Liberty* (1991).

**1993.007.** McNickle, D'Arcy. "Indians, American." *Collier's Encyclopedia: Volume 12.* New York: P. F. Collier Inc., 1993.

> On page 652, after a detailed description of the Iroquois League's founding and operation, McNickle observes: "Its political structure and idealistic conceptions contained elements that influenced liberal European philosophers of the eighteenth century and also American leaders, like Benjamin Franklin, who were searching for democratic and representative forms of government for a union of the colonies."

**1993.008.** Mitten, Lisa. [Review of Wolfson, *The Iroquois*.] *School Library Journal*, Vol. 39 (March, 1993), p. 217.

> This review of Wolfson's children's book says that it "does a good job of discussing the influence of the Iroquois Confederacy on the formation of the U.S. government."

**1993.009.** Richter, Daniel K. "Whose Indian History?" *William and Mary Quarterly* 3rd Ser. 50:2(April, 1993), pp. 379-393.

> Professor Richter is concerned, as he states in his opening sentence, that "Scholarship on the Indian peoples of early America is running out of fuel" (p. 379). Works that Richter regards as ground-breaking (such as those by William Fenton and Francis Jennings, among others) mark the "end of the line" to him (p. 380). "The predominantly white and male practitioners of the New Indian History [ethnohistory] now encounter challenges to their basic assumptions that would have been barely imaginable when the field began to flourish in the 1970s" (p. 383), which raise "questions of ownership -- of whose Indian history?" (p. 381). Among Richter's bogeymen are

"Writers and propagandists" who partake of "such modern Indian myths as the idea that whites invented scalping or the theory that the Iroquois League provided the model for the United States Constitution [who may be] charged with intellectual elitism at best and racism at worst" (p. 383). Richter names no names, except in a footnote, where *Forgotten Founders* and Johansen's 1990 exchange with Elisabeth Tooker in *Ethnohistory* are cited, as is Don Grinde's *The Iroquois and the Founding of the American Nation* (1977). Richter continues to blow a number of fuses on page 384: "Reinforcing these onslaughts against the form of Indian history that some of us had hoped would revolutionize early American studies is the scholarly and cultural *zeitgeist* traveling under the names of deconstruction, discourse theory, post-structuralism, and postmodernism." Having associated a book's worth of wildly differing ideas in the space of a page, Richter's discourse then fizzles into a rather pompous and windy dissection of these intellectual cross-currents, which he holds often "reinforce ethnic separation." (The fact that Grinde is Native American and Johansen is of European descent does not deter Richter's pell-mell rush to judgment.)

**1993.010.** Tooker, Elisabeth. [Review of *Exemplar of Liberty* (1991)]. *Northeast Anthropologist* 46(Fall, 1993), pp. 103-107.

The reviewer opens by saying that "most scholars have dismissed" Grinde's *The Iroquois and the Founding of the American Nation* (1977) and Johansen's *Forgotten Founders* (1982, 1987). She also summarily dismisses *Exemplar of Liberty*, despite the fact that "Grinde and Johansen have joined forces, greatly expanded the scope of their previous studies, and added considerably to the number of references cited." Tooker, who does not identify the scholars who purportedly agree with her, says "...[T]he result is no more convincing than their previous efforts." (p. 103) She says that Franklin did not admire the Iroquois political structure because he called Indians "ignorant savages" in his 1751 letter to James Parker in which he advised the colonists to form a union on the Iroquois model. Tooker concludes that "what Grinde and Johansen have written is an elaborate hoax...Indians were unimportant in shaping events on this continent that led up to the founding of the United States." (p. 107)

**1993.011.** Versluis, Arthur. *The Elements of Native American Traditions.* Rockport, Mass.: Shaftesbury, Dorset, 1993.

> Versluis briefly describes the Iroquois, "with their confederacy, a governmental model that, it has been suggested, served as one source of inspiration for the government adopted by the United States." (p. 11)

**1993.012.** White, John. "Canassatego, Father of Our Country: Iroquois Influence on the Founding of the United States." Minnestrista Council for Great Lakes Native American Studies, 1991-1992 Proceedings of the Woodland National Conference. Muncie, Indiana: Minnestrista Cultural Center and Ball State University, 1993.

> White, who recalls memories of Native American influence on Anglo-American democracy from his Cherokee ancestors, writes that he pursued the idea in academia to the bemusement of other scholars, who insisted that the total corpus of democracy came from the Old World. White in 1975 researched the subject in connection with an exhibit on the Iroquois in Chicago's Field Museum. White then outlines Canassatego's life, and Benjamin Franklin's appreciation of his words.

# Newspapers

**1993.013.** Endrst, James. "Turner Project Seeks to Set the Record Straight on U.S. History." Hartford *Courant*, December 3, 1993, p. B-1.

> Endrst, television critic for the *Courant*, calls Ted Turner "Television's biggest and richest idealist," as he describes the Turner series "The Native Americans." He writes that the segment "The Broken Chain" says that ideas in the U.S. Constitution were "lifted or stolen directly" from the Iroquois League, particularly the arrows on the United States Great Seal. Endrst says that "What Franklin and company did not appropriate was the [Iroquois] federation's matriarch-dominated approach to power. As [Floyd] Westerman [narrator of the series] pointed out, 'Women were the Supreme Court.'"

**1993.014.** George, Doug (Kanentiio). "Women Center of All Things Within Iroquois Society." Syracuse *Herald-American*, July

11, 1993, n.p.

> "Given the recent publication of books and articles about the
> enormous contributions of indigenous Americans to the world,
> ranging from corn to constitutions, it is most surprising to
> discover very little attention has been given to the unique role
> of women within Iroquois society," writes George.  He then
> briefly describes that role, and the influence that it had on
> nineteenth-century feminists.   It was no accident, George
> asserts, that the 1848 Seneca Falls conference, which is said to
> have founded the women's-rights movement in the United
> States, was held in Iroquois country.

**1993.015.** Kampert, Patrick.  "'Chain' Gives Native Americans
Historical Due."  Chicago *Tribune*, December 12, 1993, TV Week,
p. 3.

> This review of the Turner Broadcasting System series "The
> Native Americans" says, in part: 'The depictions of the First
> Americans' everyday life dispel the myths of single-minded
> savagery some have had of Native Americans. What can you
> learn from 'Broken Chain?'  Try these on for size: the U. S.
> borrowed some of its early ideas on government from the
> Iroquois Confederacy.  Indian chiefs are more likely  to be
> diplomats than blood-thirsty warriors....The chiefs consult a
> council of women, who give them the 'will of the people.'"

## *Other Items*

**1993.016.** Transcript #863, "Independence Day: Our Indian Legacy,"
*Larry King Live*,   Cable News Network, July 5, 1993.  With Pat
Mitchell sitting in for Larry King, the show observed Independence
Day by inviting Oren Lyons to talk about Native American precedents
for United States fundamental law.  Lyons described Iroquois consensus-
making practices, the story of the Peacemaker, and colonists' early
encounters with Native Americans that provided channels of
communication for Native American ideas.  Lyons also described the
contents of his new book *Exiled in the Land of the Free* (1992).  Lyons
described one student of his in Buffalo who was "very angry" because,
at age 32, with four children, he had never been told of the Iroquois
influence on U.S. fundamental law.  "My children are going to hear
about this," Lyons quotes the student as having said.   Lyons also
answered calls from the audience about "influence" assertions.   One
caller stressed the  importance of women in the Iroquois political

system. Lyons thanked the caller, and described ways in which Iroquois clan mothers nominate leaders in the confederacy.

**1993.017.** Transcript #351-3, Bob Cain, Cable News Network. "Native Americans had Major Role in Concept of Democracy." July 5, 1993. Television interview with Oren Lyons regarding his new book *Exiled in the Land of the Free* (1992).

**1993.018.** Internet posting: "The Friends of Ganondagan Bibliography" (http://www.ggw.org/freenet/g/ganshs/bibliog.htm) lists several books that describe the Iroquois impact on the development of democracy. Ganondagan is an Iroquois historical site and museum south of Rochester, N. Y.

**1993.019.** "Indian Pledge of Allegiance:"

> *I pledge allegiance to my tribe,*
> *To the democratic principles*
> *of the republic;*
> *and to the individual freedoms*
> *Borrowed from the Iroquois*
> *and Choctaw confederacies,*
> *As incorporated into the*
> *United States Constitution,*
> *So that my forefathers*
> *shall not have died in vain.*

The pledge was written by Lummi leader Jewell James and first read by Joseph de la Cruz, president of the Quinault Indian Nation, at the National Congress of American Indians (Tribal-states relations panel), Reno, Nevada, December 2, 1993, "dedicated to American Indian and Alaska Native veterans, leaders, people, and children."

**1993.020.** Jason Eagle. "Political Satire." 1993
[http://www.bright.net/~jeheagle/political/england.htm]
This is part of the Jason Eagle Homepage, where he says he "is attempting to bring modern science together with ancient wisdom to find a working balance." [http://www.bright.net/~jeheagle/index.html] One of Jason Eagle's satires (titled "Aristocracy vs. Democracy? England vs. Iroquois") states:

> *The English gave us Aristocracy,*
> *The Iroquois gave us Democracy.*
> *England built great Navies and sent them all over the world,*

*while the poor died in [the] streets of London.*
*No Iroquois Chief went to sleep until all of his people had*
  *eaten.*
*Which are we using today?*
*The English tax their citizens to the point of poverty.*
*The Iroquois had no word for tax.*
*Which are we using today?*
*Decide for yourself, I'm staying out of this one.*

# 1992

## Books, Scholarly, and Specialty Journals

**1992.001.** Archambault, David. [Speech to Murray, Utah Rotary Club, April 6, 1992] Reprinted in *Vital Speeches of the Day*, June 1, 1992, p. 491.

> Archambault, a Lakota and president of the United Indian College Fund, describes a number of Native American contributions to general North American culture, including "the Iroquois, for example, [who] had the world's only true democracy....It was a system that the founding fathers of the new nation would study and learn from."

**1992.002.** Berner, Robert. "American Myth: Old, New, Yet Untold." *Genre: Forms of Discourse & Culture* 25:4 (Winter, 1992), pp. 377-389.

> Berner surveys the debate over Iroquois influence on the development of American democracy in the context of the intellectual ferment over the quincentenary of Columbus' first landfall in America. Berner dismisses most of the case as evidence of "The tendency toward the creation of new legends in our revisionist era" (p. 380). "In fact," writes Berner, "the structure of matriarchal clans and League council and the council's parliamentary procedures bear no resemblance whatever to the structure of the Constitution" (p. 381). With his mind set in such a manner, Berner finds Johansen's assertion that the Iroquois structure of "younger brothers" and "older brothers" resembled a two-house legislature "rather limp" (p. 382), although "his claims for generally [*sic*] Indian influences

on the development of American notions of political freedom proceed from a premise that is worth considering" (p. 382). *Forgotten Founders* and Donald Grinde's 1993 piece in *AICRJ* are cited.

**1992.003.** Brennan, Terry. "Natural Rights and the Constitution: The Original 'Original Intent.'" *Harvard Journal of Law and Public Policy.* Vol. 15 (1992), p. 1029.

> In a footnote (number 252), Brennan speculates that the right of privacy may be rooted in the Iroquois Great Law of Peace as well as in European precedents.

**1992.004.** Delgado, Richard. "Rodrigo's Chronicle." *Yale Law Journal* 101 (Spring, 1992), p. 1357.

> In this review of Dinesh D'Souza's *Illiberal Education: the Politics of Race and Sex on Campus* [1991], Delgado, a law professor at the University of Colorado, lists a number of books on various multicultural themes that serve to refute D'Souza's arguments. He has a section on "Essays and books on the influence of American Indian ideas on the U.S. Constitution" which includes Felix Cohen's essay "Americanizing the White Man," (1952), Johansen, *Forgotten Founders* (1982, 1987), and Weatherford, *Indian Givers* (1988).

**1992.005.** Hoeveler, J. David, Jr. "Original Intent and the Politics of Republicanism." *Marquette Law Review* 75 (Summer, 1992), p. 863.

> Hoeveler, chair of the history department at the University of Wisconsin, Milwaukee, is discussing liberal and conservative interpretations of the doctrine of original intent. In this context, he discusses Arthur Schlesinger, Jr.'s arguments in *Disuniting of America* [1992]. In a footnote, Hoeveler mentions the New York State "Curriculum of Inclusion," asserting that "the curriculum guide for American history demanded that that the 'Haudensaunee' [*sic*] (Iroquois) political system be acknowledged as influencing the development of the American Constitution."

**1992.006.** Malloy, Robin Paul. "Letters From the Longhouse: Law, Economics, and Native American Values." *Wisconsin Law Review* (September/October, 1992), p. 1569.

These are personal reflections of Malloy, who is a Kahnawake Mohawk and Professor of Law and Economics at the Syracuse University School of Law. Malloy notes that the United States Senate and House of Representatives have passed resolutions recognizing Iroquois contributions to United States fundamental law. This piece outlines the origins and procedures of the Iroquois confederacy, and cites articles in *Northeast Indian Quarterly* by Grinde (1987, 1989), as well as another article by Robert W. Venables in the same publication (1987). Malloy writes that "...Upon the shores of Onondaga Lake...democracy in its purist form flourished among the Haudenosaunee a thousand years...these first citizens of liberty enjoyed the freedom of religion, expression, conscience, speech, movement, and all the other freedoms that we all take for granted." Malloy makes an unattributed statement that "one third of the United States Constitution can be traced back to the five Iroquois nations' form of government." The bibliography of this article lists Johansen, *Forgotten Founders* (1982, 1987).

**1992.007.** Weintraub, David. "Iroquois Influence in the Founding of the American Nation." *Court Review* 29 (Winter, 1992) pp. 17-32.

This is a very detailed summary of the Iroquois League and ways in which it helped to shape American concepts of democracy. Weintraub, a third-year law student at Touro College Jacob D. Fuchsberg Law Center, used this piece to win first prize in the American Judges Association/American Judges Foundation 1992 Law Student Essay Contest.

## Newspapers and Trade Magazines

**1992.008.** _____. "Feminist Connection to Iroquois Topic of SUNY Oswego Program." *The Valley News*, November 9, 1992.

Page 15: Announcement of a presentation by Sally Roesch Wagner on "The Iroquois influence in the 19th century women's-rights movement," Nov. 18, at the State University of New York/Oswego, sponsored by the student government. Similar articles appeared November 12 in *The Oswegonian News*, and November 16 in the Syracuse *Post-Standard's* Oswego section.

**1992.009.** Cojean, Annick. "Desarrois Americains IX. Historie: du 'Melting Pot' au Saladier." *Le Monde* (Paris) October 30, 1992.

> Cojean describes the debate over multicultural education in the United States, raising, as an example, "De l'influence du modele Iroquois."

**1992.010.** Hornback, Bert G. "The Paradise He and His Followers Destroyed." Louisville *Courier-Journal*, October 11, 1992, p. 1-D.

> In this opinion piece, "he" is Christopher Columbus. Hornback, a professor of humanities at Bellermine College, writes that Columbus' voyages began an invasion that uprooted cultures which in some ways were superior to those of Europe. Without the European invasion, Native Americans might never have had electric hot-dog cookers, 9,000-decibel stereos, or atomic bombs, but, "Before we came...the Native Americans we call the Iroquois were the founders of what was called the Great Law of Peace....Benjamin Franklin thought the Great Law was the finest model of government he had seen, and recommended the Iroquois federation as a model for the new white nation about to be formed."

**1992.011.** Innerst, Carol. "Cut and Paste History: 'PC' Texts Drop Some Big Names." Washington *Times*, April 26, 1992, p. 1.

> This lengthy front-page piece asserts that many school children can no longer identify Nathan Hale as they strive "to integrate the long-slighted experiences of women and members of minorities into a new and multicultural vision of Americans' heritage." As one example of this change, Innerst cites a textbook published in 1950 (*America's History*) on the Albany Plan of Union (1754) with *Triumph of the American Nation* (1986), which says: "The example of the Iroquois Confederation had an influence on Benjamin Franklin and his efforts to promote an intercolonial union."

**1992.012.** Maybury-Lewis, David. "Tribal Wisdom: Is It Too Late to Reclaim the Benefits of Tribal Living?" *Utne Reader*, July/August 1992, pp. 68-95.

> On pages 76-77, in the context of a discussion of African tribes thrown together in European-designated nations, a sidebar

notes that: "There has been intriguing talk in Uganda of a confederation of tribes based on the League of the Iroquois, where local power would be left to the tribes and state politics would be decided by a joint council in which each tribe, regardless of size, has an equal vote." This is a sidebar to the main article by Jason W. Clay, originally published in *Mother Jones*, November/December, 1990. Maybury-Lewis ends this article calling for a "new federalism, which, after the manner of the League of the Iroquois, permits each people in the nation to keep its council fire alight," The Great Law, writes Maybury-Lewis, "was remarkable because it was a constitution that had the force of a religion." (p. 79)

## *Other Items*

**1992.013.**   Oren Lyons, an Onondaga member of the Iroquois Grand Council, appeared on "Bill Moyers' Journal" (Public Broadcasting Service), July 4, 1992; he discussed Iroquois ecological and political traditions, and asserted Iroquoian precedents for United States government.

**1992.014.** Transcript, "Notes for a Speech by the Right Honorable Joe Clark...President of the Privy Council and Minister Responsible for Constitutional Affairs." [At the annual meeting of the Canadian Manufacturer's Association] Toronto, June 12, 1992. In LEXIS. Clark addresses the problems of Canadian nationhood as they impinge on the present constitutional debate in that country. Clark asserts the right and ability of Native Canadians to govern themselves, pointing to the Iroquois: "Aboriginal self-government...was here when Thomas Jefferson and Benjamin Franklin looked to the Iroquois Confederacy when they were designing the American Constitution."

**1992.015.**   Videotape, "More Than Bows and Arrows," one hour, described in catalogue of Insight Media, New York City: "This award-winning documentary illuminates the impact that Native Americans have had on the political, social, and cultural development of the U.S. Narrated by N. Scott Momaday, it examines how government, agriculture and food, transportation, architecture, science, and technology, the arts, medicine, and language all have benefitted from Native American contributions."

**1992.016.**   "Bad Magic: The Failure of Technology."
[http://www.ratical.com/ratville/AoS/theSun.html]
"An Interview with Jerry Mander by Catherine Ingram, published in

*The Sun* (a journal of opinion), date not provided; posted to the Internet in 1992. Ingram, quoting Mander: "In the case of Western industrial countries, Indians are viewed fundamentally as of the past, out of date; primitive in the negative sense, meaning unable to sustain governments or societies, unable to think great thoughts, contribute to Western ideas, or leave behind beautiful architecture. They're criticized in all the areas that we think we are good in. But there is substantial evidence that the philosophical basis of the U.S. Constitution comes from the Great Binding Law of the Iroquois, which goes back at least to the 1500s; the Iroquois say it goes back a thousand years before that. The Great Binding Law is a system of egalitarian, federated governance with absolute democracy and strong checks and balances, and it actually continues to exist in some ways at present. Now the U.S. Constitution must have borrowed many of those principles because there were no other democratic and federated models available in the world at that time."

## *Scholarly Meetings and Public Forums*

**1992.017.** [January, 1992] University of Nebraska at Omaha. Johansen lectured on the debate surrounding the "influence issue" on the occasion of his promotion to full professor, at a reception hosted by the UNO College of Arts & Sciences.

**1992.018.** [April, 1992] Four to five thousand citizens of Kansas City observed Earth Day by assembling a very large mosaic of materials to be recycled in the shape of a turtle, after the Iroquois reference to North America as "Turtle Island." The mosaic, which occupied roughly the space of a football field, was constructed in a Kansas City park, and dismantled the next day. Information on Iroquois life, including constitutional influence, was distributed at the event. Organizer Marty Kraft provided an aerial photograph of the turtle mosaic with participants circling it.

**1992.019.** [April, 1992] Grinde and Johansen presented papers based on *Exemplar of Liberty* at the Organization of American Historians annual meeting in Chicago.

**1992.020.** [October, 1992] Johansen presented a paper, "Roger Williams, 'Soul Liberty,' and the Native Peoples of New England," at a conference called to air Native American viewpoints on the Columbian Quincentenary, University of California at Los Angeles.

# 1991

## *Books, Scholarly, and Specialty Journals*

**1991.001.** _____. [Review: Mander, *In the Absence of the Sacred*, 1991.] *Et Cetera* 49:2(Summer, 1992), pp. 247-248.

> In addition to describing Native Americans' sense of the sacred, this review says that Mander discusses "their system[s] of government (especially the Great Binding Law of the Iroquois Confederacy) and [its] influence on the political philosophies of Franklin, Madison, and Jefferson..."

**1991.002.** _____. "Iroquois Women and the Early Suffragists [is] Topic Selected for Stanton Tea Presentation." *Elizabeth Cady Stanton Foundation* [Newsletter, Seneca Falls, N.Y.], Autumn, 1991, n.p.

> "Noted scholar and feminist Sally Roesch Wagner and Native American activist [and clan mother] Audrey Shenandoah will be the featured speakers at the annual tea in honor of the birth of Elizabeth Cady Stanton on Sunday, November 10, at 4 p.m. at the Gould Hotel in Seneca Falls." Seneca Falls was the site of a conference in 1848 that is said to have founded modern feminism as a social movement in the United States. This article notes that, "In 1848, before coming to [the] Seneca Falls [conference], Lucretia Mott [an important women's-rights advocate], visited with women of the Iroquois Nation." Wagner and Shenandoah will lecture on the ways in which Iroquois women and their sociopolitical milieu helped shape early feminism of Mott, Stanton, and Matilda Joslyn Gage.

**1991.003.** Davidson, James W., and Michael B. Stoff. *The American Nation*. Englewood Cliffs, N.J.: Prentice-Hall, 1991.

> On page 47, this grade-school text asserts that the opening words of the U.S. Constitution, "We the People," have an Iroquois origin.

**1991.004.** Delgado, Richard and Jean Stefancic. "Norms and Narratives: Can Judges Avoid Serious Moral Error?" *Texas Law Review* 69 (June, 1991), p. 1929.

Delgado and Stefancic write that "Many colonial leaders, including Benjamin Franklin, championed the Indians' cause," as they describe "the 'constitutional' system of the Iroquois, a system the influence of which on Benjamin Franklin was freely acknowledged by him." Delgado is Charles Inglis professor of law at the University of Colorado; Stefancic is a legal librarian at the San Francisco University School of Law.

**1991.005.** Dorris, Michael and Louise Erdrich. *The Crown of Columbus: A Novel.* New York: HarperCollins, 1991.

On page 83, the narrator, Vivian Two Star, asserts to a white academic, "A third of the medicines we use today were developed over here long before the fifteenth century. Not to mention the Iroquois concept of representative government or the Equal Rights Amendment."

**1991.006.** Jan Maher and Doug Selwyn, *Native Americans: Grades 3 and 4.* Seattle: Turman Publishing, 1991.

Pages 15-16 of this elementary-school workbook discuss the Iroquois Great Law of Peace, Benjamin Franklin, and the writing of the Constitution, including role of the Albany Congress of 1754, during which Franklin and other colonial leaders met with Iroquois sachems.

**1991.007.** Mander, Jerry. "Our Founding Mothers and Fathers, the Iroquois." *Earth Island Journal* 6:4(Fall, 1991), pp. 30-33.

This article is an excerpt from Mander's *In the Absence of the Sacred* (1991), describing the Iroquois Confederacy's structure and history, and ways in which it helped shape United States political traditions. Mander writes that the Iroquois Great Law of Peace was "arguably the most important single model" for the Albany Plan of 1754, the Articles of Confederation, and the U. S. Constitution. Grinde's *The Iroquois and the Founding of the American Nation* is cited.

**1991.008.** Newman, Frank C. "The Randolph W. Thrower Symposium: Comparative Constitutionalism...." *Emory Law Journal* 40 (Summer, 1991), p. 731.

This is the printed text of remarks by Newman during a symposium at Emory University, in which he discusses the U.S.

Bill of Rights and other, similar concepts. He notes that
"...Colonial leaders learned about the Iroquois government at
treaty councils....They returned with a taste for natural rights
(life, liberty, and happiness) that they saw operating on the
other side of the frontier." Newman, now retired, was Jackson
H. Ralston Professor of International Law at the University of
California--Berkeley and a justice of the California Supreme
Court. He cites Maria Morocco's piece in the American Bar
Association publication *Human Rights* (1990). She is quoting
Johansen at the American Bar Association annual meeting of
August, 1990, in Chicago.

**1991.009.** Oliver, Revilo P. "Scalping the Unwary." *Liberty Bell
Magazine,* July, 1991.
[http://www2.stormfront.org/rpo/scalping.htm]

*Liberty Bell* is a house organ of "Storm Front: The White
Nationalist Resource Page," which comes on screen with a
logotype reading "White Pride, World Wide." Revilo
complains that, "At this moment, New York's 11th-grade
history syllabus tells teachers that the two major influences on
the U.S. Constitution were the European Enlightenment of the
seventeenth and eighteenth centuries and the political system
of the Haudenosaunee Indians....[T]he...claim is sheer nonsense.
Of course, the notion that the authors of the Constitution would
have taken into consideration a league of savages, about which
they knew little...is simply preposterous and shows only the
total dishonesty of the racketeers who operate the public boob-
hatcheries."

Revilo continues: "By the way, the hogwash about the
Constitution was obviously derived, not from the presumptuous
Indians, but directly from Communist doctrine. Morgan's book
about the Hodenosaunee [*sic*] came to the attention of Marx
while he was looking for sources he could plausibly cite in
apparent support of his Marxian Reformation of Christianity,
and it was used as a major source by Marx's employer and
accomplice, Engels, when he compounded Bolshevik hokum for
his *Origin of the Family, Private Property, and the State,*
which became the fundamental textbook of the Judaeo-
Communist conspiracy."

He concludes: "As for the [New York State] "Curriculum of
Inclusion," it represents a larger plan to rework the history

curriculum in order to accommodate various political pressure groups. The goal, as [Thomas] Sobol's task force makes clear, is to reduce the 'arrogance' of 'European American' (i.e., white) students."

**1991.010.** Shenandoah, Audrey. "Women: Sustainers of Life." *Turtle Quarterly* [Niagara Falls, N.Y.], Summer, 1990, pp. 5-10.

Shenandoah, an Onondaga clan mother, describes the role of women in Iroquois society, as well as the influence of that role on non-Iroquois women: "Reading and working with women from around the world, I have met with several white women who don't feel that it's at all coincidental that most of the women's movements began around what is now central New York....[T]hey are beginning to feel and see in their research that they [suffragists] did in fact follow the pattern of what they saw was already here, the Houdenosaunee. Women's suffrage began in central New York."

**1991.011.** Worthen, Kevin J. "Essay: Two Sides of the Same Coin: The Potential Normative Power of American Cities and Indian Tribes." *Vanderbilt Law Review* 44 (November, 1991), p. 1273.

Worthen, associate professor in the Brigham Young University School of Law, mentions the Iroquois political system and its influence on American democracy as an aside in his comparison of tribal and urban governance. He cites Bagley and Ruckman (1983).

## *Newspapers and Magazines*

**1991.012.** Davidson, Nicholas. "Was Socrates a Plagiarist?" *National Review* 43:3(Feb. 25, 1991), p. 45.

This piece is mainly a critique of Afrocentric education, but it begins: "Shakespeare and Locke are non-gratae at Stanford; New York schoolchildren learn that the Iroquois were the real source of the Constitution. Multiculturalism is on the march."

**1991.013.** Koehler, Robert. "Moyers Explores Spirit of Indian Faith Keeper." Los Angeles *Times*, July 8, 1991, p. F-9.

This is a review of Bill Moyers' interview with Oren Lyons, which was broadcast on the Public Broadcasting System July 3. Koehler, who characterizes Lyons as "a down-to-earth sage," describes how the Onondaga faithkeeper "takes...us through the tale of the founding of the Six Nations, or Iroquois Confederation, how this union not only established a democratic peace-keeping forum, but how it deeply influenced Benjamin Franklin, Thomas Jefferson, and other framers of the Declaration of Independence."

**1991.014.** Mander, Jerry.   "What You Don't Know About Indians." *Utne Reader*, November-December 1991, pp. 67-74.

In this excerpt from his book *In the Absence of the Sacred*, Mander writes that lack of instruction about Native American governmental systems is a failing of American education. "Some of them, notably the Iroquois, apparently had considerable effect on concepts later incorporated into the Articles of Confederation and Constitution." Mander writes as he mentions concepts of "checks and balances, popular participation in decision-making, direct representation, states' rights, and bicameral legislatures, all of which were part of the Great Binding Law of the Iroquois Confederacy."

**1991.015.** Pierre, Henri.  "L'offensive de la 'Afrocentrisme.'" *Le Monde* (Paris), March 7, 1991.

Pierre describes debates over multicultural history in the United States, particularly Afrocentric ideas that are being used in various school districts. He also briefly describes the debate in the New York State of Department of Education guide *Haudenosaunee: Past, Present, Future* that Iroquois precedent helped shape the origins of democracy in the United States. "La tache n'est pas facile," he writes.  "Etant donnee l'importance de la pression des groupes ethniques....inclure cette affirmation que le systeme politique des Iroquois a influence... redaction de la Constitution des Etats-Unis."

**1991.016.** Taylor, Jared. [Review, Clifton, *Invented Indian*, 1991] *American Renaissance* [Louisville, Kentucky], December, 1990, n.p.

Taylor agrees lavishly with Clifton's belief that Native Americans had no environmental or egalitarian ethic, calling such arguments part of an ahistorical, sentimental myth. Part

of what he calls "the great Indian myth" is "that early
Americans learned about democracy and the advantages of
unity by studying the Iroquois Confederacy." Taylor says that
Clifton "explodes" this "myth."

## Other Items

**1991.017.** Announcement of *Exemplar of Liberty* in newsletter of the
Nebraska State Council for the Social Studies, May 5, 1991. Published
in Omaha, NE.

**1991.018.** Internet posting: David Yarrow, "Resources on Iroquois
Democracy and Government," NativeNet (Native-L@Tamvm1.bitnet),
1991.

# 1990

## Books, Scholarly and Specialty Journals

**1990.001.** Alfred, Gerald. [Review of Sharon O'Brien, *American
Indian Tribal Governments*, 1989] *Northeast Indian Quarterly*
7:1(Spring, 1990), pp. 38-39.

> Alfred, on page 38, criticizes O'Brien for overstating and
> simplifying the Iroquois' contributions to democracy. O'Brien,
> on page 50 of her book, says that "Franklin modelled the new
> country's structure after that of the Iroquois League." Instead,
> writes Alfred, she should have written that Franklin observed
> the Iroquois, was influenced by their system, and factored the
> Iroquois example into his ideas as one of several examples.
> "The United States Constitution is a document influenced by a
> host of ideas," Alfred writes. (p. 38) "I doubt many
> Haudenosaunee (Iroquois) would accept the blame for spawning
> the complex and contradictory legislative, judicial, and
> bureaucratic structures that characterize the American
> system." (p. 38)

**1990.002.** MacLaine, Craig and Michael S. Baxendale. *This Land
is Our Land: The Mohawk Revolt at Oka.* Montreal: Optimum
Publishing International, 1990.

> In this journalistic account of the confrontation at Kanesatake

(Oka) and Kahnawake during 1990, Louis Hall, founder of the Mohawk Warrior Society, is quoted on page 65 as saying: "There has been a 300 year dark age for the Great Law of Peace. It was used frequently in the writing of the Constitution of the United States of America but there is little knowledge of it among non-Natives....The white man has always tried to eliminate the Longhouse law and replace it with his Indian Act." In the same volume, on page 87, "Dale," a clan mother of the Mohawk Bear Clan, is quoted as saying: "One aspect of the Iroquois Law that was not copied (in the American Constitution)...established women's rights. Now Americans are trying to pass an equal-rights amendment because they ignored the equality of women two hundred years ago." On pages 99 and 100, in the introduction of a condensed version of the Great Law, the authors write: "When the founding fathers of the United States of America were writing the constitution of their newly-established country, they borrowed liberally from the Great Law. The Senate acknowledged this in 1987."

**1990.003.** Morocco, Maria. "Rediscovering the Roots of American Democracy." *Human Rights*, Vol. 17 No. 3 (Fall, 1990), pp. 38-39.

Morocco covered the panel on the Iroquois and democracy at the American Bar Association 1990 convention for the event's daily newspaper. In this article, she develops material from the panel at greater length in *Human Rights*, citing Grinde, Kickingbird, Lyons, and Johansen from the ABA panel. *Human Rights* is published by the Amnerican Bar Association in Chicago, where Morocco was a copy editor in 1990.

**1990.004.** Ravitch, Diane. "Multiculturalism: E Pluribus Plures." *American Scholar* 59 (1990), pp. 337-354.

Ravitch, adjunct professor of history and education at Teacher's College, Columbia University, surveys disputes related to multicultural education, bringing into her ambit the *Haudenosaunee: Past, Present, Future* curriculum then being assembled in New York State. She believes that assertions of Iroquois influence on American democracy in this curriculum is "filiopietism and ethnic boosterism" (p. 347), which she says have taken place in New York State because of Iroquois political influence. Ravitch's line of reasoning is borrowed nearly verbatim by Schlesinger in *Disuniting of America* (1992).

**1990.005.** Williams, Robert A., Jr. "Gendered Checks and Balances: Understanding the Legacy of White Patriarchy in an American Indian Cultural Context." *Georgia Law Review* 24 (1990), p. 1019.

> The main emphasis of this article is ways in which women's legal and political roles differ in Iroquois and some other indigenous societies *vis a vis* mainstream American culture. Williams mentions the "influence" issue as an aside, citing Grinde (1977) and Johansen (1982, 1987).

## Newspapers

**1990.006.** Pareles, Jon. "American Indian Music Helps a Culture Hold On." New York *Times*, December 4, 1990, p. C-15.

> This is a feature on the Akwesasne Mohawk Singers, who were scheduled to perform the same evening at Weill Recital Hall. Pareles writes: "The songs and dances offer glimpses of nations far more venerable than the United States. The Iroquois Confederation...'was the first United Nations, united for peace,' said Mr. [Brad] Bonaparte. He added that the form of government of the United States was influenced by the Great Law of the Iroquois, whose system of delegates and representatives was studied by Benjamin Franklin and Thomas Jefferson."

**1990.007.** Schrader, Andrea. "Rights of Women Discussed." [Oswego] *Palladium-Times*, March 26, 1990.

> This is a report on a lecture by Sally Roesch Wagner at the Upstate New York Women's History Organization conference at the State University of New York/Oswego. Wagner lectured on the ways in which Matilda Joslyn Gage and other early feminists were influenced by the social system of the Iroquois. "Iroquois women could own property and hold important political and religious positions in a time white women could only dream of such things," Schrader reports Wagner to have said.

**1990.008.** Stout, J. Dean. "Finding Kindred Spirits is the Key." Lewiston [Idaho] *Morning Tribune,* July 7, 1990, p. 5-B.

> Stout, of the United Methodist Church, is writing on the anniversary of the Declaration of Independence. Stout says that within the last year he discovered that Benjamin Franklin "said they [the signers of the declaration] had searched the governments of ancient and contemporary Asian and European nations and found no form of government suitable. The pattern from which they found the three-department system they used was the Great Law of Peace of the Iroquois Indians....I discover my Indian friends have known this for years, but it was not in t he history I studied in school."

# 1989

## *Books, Scholarly, and Other Journals*

**1989.001.** _____. "Applauding Our Constitution: Hands-on Creative Lessons." Winston-Salem, N.C.: Center for Research and Development in Law-related Education, 1989.

> This is a handbook of 28 lesson plans for teachers focussed on the U.S. Constitution. One of the lesson plans is titled: "The Haudenosaunee (Iroquois) and the U.S. Constitution..."

**1989.002.** Ball, Milner S. "Legal Storytelling: Stories of Origin and Constitutional Possibilities." *Michigan Law Review* 87 (August, 1989), p. 2280.

> Milner Ball, Caldwell Professor of Constitutional Law at the University of Georgia School of Law, writes in footnote #85 that American Indian tribes existed as legal entities "long before the state and federal governments were formed." He notes "persuasive evidence that American democracy began between 350 and 500 years before the American Revolution with the Iroquois Law of the Great Peace." Ball uses this fact to support his assertion that "...Tribes, unlike local governments, have inherent authority to govern; they need not rely on outside legislative power to give them authority to act." He cites Bagley and Ruckman (1983).

**1989.003.** Fadden, Ray (Tehanetorens). "Migration of the Iroquois." Joseph Bruchac, ed. *New Voices From the Longhouse.* Greenfield Center, N. Y.: Greenfield Review Press, 1989, pp. 99-104.

> Page 103: "Also, white leaders watched the operation of the Iroquois government and learned union and democracy from it. Historians are now beginning to admit what they must have known a long time ago -- that the government of the United States is not patterned after something across the ocean...but it is patterned after the government of the people of the Longhouse, where all people -- women as well as men -- are represented and control their government."

**1989.004.** McClard, Megan and George Ypsilantis. *Hiawatha and the Iroquois League.* Alvin Josephy's Biography Series of American Indians. Englewood Cliffs, N.J.: Silver Burdett Press/Simon & Schuster, 1989.

> This book for young people outlines the life of Hiawatha (Aionwanta), co-founder of the League of the Haudenosaunee with the Peacemaker. The authors also outline the history of the League and its effects on subsequent history, including the United States federal system and the writings of Marx and Engels. On p. xii, the authors write that "many perceptive white people thought it [the Iroquois League] was more democratic and representative of its people than any government then existing in Europe. In fact, there are those who believe that the League made a deep impression on Benjamin Franklin and other founders of America's constitutional form of government." This theme arises again on pp. 120 and 121; the Iroquois' impact of Marx and Engels, through Lewis Henry Morgan's writings, is developed on pp. 116 and 118.

**1989.005.** Mohawk, John. "Origins of Iroquois Political Thought," in Joseph Bruchac, ed. *New Voices From the Longhouse.* Greenfield Center, N. Y.: Greenfield Review Press, 1989, pp. 218-228.

> Page 226: "Europeans [in America]...learned to think in egalitarian terms....They began to adopt the custom of democratic social ideals; they became healthy skeptics in the way that Indian people showed them....This way of thinking

was the most powerful change Europe experienced in the Americas. It was to change the face of Europe and the world forever."

**1989.006.** O'Brien, Sharon. *American Indian Tribal Governments.* Norman: University of Oklahoma Press, 1989.

> On page 50 of this legal textbook, O'Brien (having outlined the structure and operations of the Iroquois League on pp. 18-20) writes that "Benjamin Franklin had modelled the new country's structure [in the Articles of Confederation] on that of the Iroquois League." She points out that the loose confederacy that had served the Iroquois so well "was ineffective for the United States." On page 46, O'Brien also quotes Canassatego at the Lancaster Treaty Council (1744), and Benjamin Franklin's letter to James Parker (1751) on colonial emulation of the Iroquois union. O'Brien lists Grinde, *Iroquois and the Founding of the American Nation* (1977) in her bibliography (p. 324).

**1989.007.** Resnik, Judith. "Dependent Sovereigns: Indian Tribes, States, and the Federal Courts." *University of Chicago Law Review* 56 (Spring, 1989), p. 671.

> Resnik, a professor of law at the University of Southern California, argues Indians' right and ability to govern themselves, observing that "Indian tribes, such as the Iroquois Confederacy, had a structure of government that predated and may have influenced the drafting of the United States Constitution." In footnote 215, she cites Johansen, *Forgotten Founders* (1982, 1987).

## Newspapers

**1989.008.** Ames, Lynne. "Interfaith Chapter Marks its 30th Year." New York *Times* [Westchester Weekly Desk], p. 12-WC, May 7, 1989.

> This is an interview with Margaret Gilmore, executive director of the New York Region's National Conference of Christians and Jews, who founded the group's Westchester Chapter thirty years ago. The group has been running a series of seminars on multicultural subjects. In the fall, the seminars will take up American Indian history, including Iroquois influence on

democracy. "People learn things they may not have known," William Jordan, director of the program, is quoted as saying. "Thomas Jefferson and Benjamin Franklin sat down with the Iroquois chiefs and modelled much of this country's new government on the Iroquois government."

**1989.009.** Folkdal, Kirsten. "Democracy in U. S. Affected by Iroquois, Says Speaker." *The California Aggie*, December 4, 1989, p. 3.

This is a report on a joint lecture by Donald A. Grinde, Jr. and Sally Roesch Wagner, who "presented their new research and challenged the concept that the United States imported its governmental system and women's rights tradition from Europe," before an audience of about 100. Grinde's speech was drawn from material that was later published in *Exemplar of Liberty* (1991). Wagner detailed how women activists at the 1848 Seneca Falls Conference had earlier associated with Iroquois clan mothers and observed their pivotal role in Iroquois political society.

# 1988

## *Book*

**1988.001.** Landsman, Gail. *Sovereignty and Symbol: Indian-White Conflict at Ganienkeh.* Albuquerque: University of New Mexico Press, 1988.

On pp. 195-203, in an appendix, Landsman reprints the "Ganienkeh Manifesto," distributed by Mohawks who started their own settlement during 1974 on a 612-acre site in the Adirnacks. On page 199, the manifesto compares the preamble of the Constitution of the United Nations with wording from the beginning of the Iroquois Great Law of Peace, a comparison that is borrowed from Wallace, *Great Law of Peace* (1945). The manifesto comments (on p. 200): "*Gayanerekowa* [The Great Law of Peace] was the world's first national constitution and the first international law, the first code of human rights. The Iroquois Confederacy was the world's first people's republic."

# *Magazine*

**1988.002.** Johansen, Bruce E.  "American Indian History" [Letter to the Editor].  *The New Republic,*  December 19, 1988, p. 4.

> Replying to Michael Newman's dismissal of the "influence" idea in *The New Republic's* November 7, 1988 issue, Johansen writes that the "good news" for Newman is that the Founders did not "copy" the Constitution from the Iroquois. The bad news for him is that "American Indian confederacies did help shape the thoughts of our founders, most notably Benjamin Franklin and Thomas Jefferson." The biggest historical myth of all, writes Johansen, is that "our 'new republic' was cut entirely from European cloth."

# *Other Item*

**1988.003.** "You're Looking at the First Draft of the Constitution," Public service advertisement for American Indian Arts and Amerinda, New York City.  Created by Drossman Lehman Marino Advertising Agency, New York City.  This piece, which ran in *People* and *Newsweek,* depicts an Iroquois wampum belt and discusses Franklin and Jefferson's views on native governance.  Copy from *Advertising Age,* "Global Gallery: Creative Advertising From Around the World," October 10, 1988.

# *Scholarly Conferences and Public Events*

**1988.004.** Program, "The Living Constitution," University of South Dakota, Vermillion, October 5-6, 1988.  Johansen delivered a presentation at this event, which was later published. (*Akwesasne Notes,* 1991). He also met briefly with Warren Burger, retired Chief Justice of the U. S. Supreme Court and Chairman of the U.S. Bicentennial Commission, who was the conference's keynote speaker.

**1988.005.** Gail Landsman, "Portrayals of the Iroquois in the Woman Suffrage Movement," Paper presented at the annual Conference on Iroquois Research, Rensselaerville, New York, October 8, 1988.

# 1987

## *Scholarly Journal*

**1987.001.** Delgado, Richard. "Review Essay: Derrick Bell and the Ideology of Racial Reform: Will We Ever Be Saved." *Yale Law Journal* 97 (1988), p. 923.

>  Most of this review essay is concerned with the intractable nature of racial tension in American society. Delgado finds that civil-rights law usually acts only as a corrective for minorities when it runs congruent with established interests. Delgado says that the books of Derrick Bell, a professor of law at Harvard, bear this out. As an aside, Delgado writes that "Although books praising the Constitution and tracing the origins of its miraculous ideas generally neglect to mention this fact, some of the ideas in our form of government came from the Iroquois. Before Columbus 'discovered' America, the Five Nations of the Iroquois had formed a constitutional confederation based on a document called the Great Law of Peace...." Delgado then lists a summary of similarities, citing Johansen, *Forgotten Founders* (1982, 1987).

## *Newspaper and Magazine*

**1987.002.** _____. "Framers Took Some Cues From Iroquois System." Minneapolis *Star-Tribune*, June 1, 1987, p. 1-A, 14-A.

>  This front-page article details assertions of Iroquois contributions to democracy, from Johansen, *Forgotten Founders* (1982, 1987). It provides a lengthy description of ways in which Benjamin Franklin, Thomas Jefferson, and other colonial and early United States leaders interacted with the Iroquois and borrowed ideas from them.

**1987.003.** Spense, Cathie Slater. "In Search of the April Fool." *Yankee* [magazine], April, 1987, p. 154.

>  This brief piece summarizes the life of William James Sidis, reputed prodigy, who, in 1914 at the age of 16, became Harvard University's youngest graduate. Mention is made of Boston resident Dan Mahoney's discovery of Sidis' unpublished manuscript, *Tribes and States*, which maintains that

immigrants from Europe to New England learned many of their democratic institutions from the Penacook federation, which had borrowed them from the Iroquois.

## *Other Items*

**1987.004.** Two "Field Workbook Leaflets," with text and artwork by John Kahionhes Fadden, "a service of the Young Worker Program...of the New York State Historical Association." The leaflets, both titled "Native Americans in New York State: Symbols of the Haudenosaunee," outlines ways in which European colonists adopted some of the symbols and ideas of the Iroquois.

**1987.005.** Public Relations Newswire, December 17, 1987, in LEXIS. "Kirke Kickingbird Receives Bicentennial Award." The Institute for the Development of Indian Law will give an award to Kickingbird for outstanding contributions to the bicentennial of the U.S. Constitution. the award is based in part on his creation of a 36-page booklet, "Indians and the U.S. Constitution," along with a brochure and 15-minute video.

**1987.006.** David Yarrow. "The Great Law of Peace: New World Roots of American Democracy." [http://www.danwinter.com/yarrow/grtlaw.html] Sept., 1987. One vital perspective has been missing from the pageantry regarding the bicentennial of the U.S. Constitution, writes Yarrow, "for the true historical origins of freedom and democracy in the New World -- and indeed, in modern civilization itself -- lie nearly forgotten on the pages of time, where they were written centuries before the days of King George and the Founding Fathers of the United States Constitution.   Perhaps, amidst the revelry, we will take this opportunity to turn back these pages, to rediscover and possibly fulfill our debt to one of the great social wonders of history: The Great Law of Peace." Yarrow also reviews the conference at Cornell University (September, 1987) on the Great Law of Peace and the U.S. Constitution.

## *Conferences and Public Events*

**1987.007.** [September 11-12] Cornell University, "Cultural Encounter: the Iroquois Great Law of Peace and the United States Constitution," Cornell American Indian Program, *et  a l.* Proceedings were published; see Jose Barreiro, ed., *Indian Roots of American Democracy* (1988).

**1987.008.** [November 27] Johansen spoke to a gathering convened by E. David Griffith, an attorney, at the Trianon of Colorado Springs School, for debate and discussion on ideas in *Forgotten Founders*.

**1987.009.** [December 2] Hearing, U.S. Senate Select Committee on Indian Affairs, on S. Con. Res. 76, "To acknowledge the contribution of the Iroquois Confederacy of Nations to the development of the United States Constitution..." The hearing was held in Washington, D.C. A transcript is available.

# 1975 - 1986

## *All Sources*

**1975.001.** _____. "Haudenosaunee Statement to the World," *Akwesasne Notes*, 11 (May, 1979), p. 7.

> The Chiefs of the Iroquois confederacy reiterate their longstanding traditional opinion that "European people left our council fires and journeyed forth into the world to spread principles of justice and democracy which they learned from us and which have had profound effects upon the evolution of the Modern World." (p. 7)

**1975.002.** Akwesasne Notes, ed. *Basic Call to Consciousness*. (1978) Rooseveltown, N.Y., 1986.

> On pages 11 and 54, this booklet describing the speeches of a Haudenosaunee delegation to the United Nations in Geneva (1977) compares the League of the Iroquois to the United Nations. Page 11: "When the idea of a United Nations of the world was proposed toward the end of World War II, researchers were dispatched to find models in history for such an organization. For all practical purposes, the only model they found concerned the Constitution of the Five Nations..." p. 54: "[T]he Great Law of Peace....is the oldest functioning document in the world which has contained a recognition of the freedoms that Western democracies recently claim as their own."

**1975.003.** Aquila, Richard. *The Iroquois Restoration: Iroquois Diplomacy on the Colonial Frontier*, 1701-1754. Detroit: Wayne State University Press, 1983.

> On page 191, Aquila cites Canassatego's advice to colonial representatives that the colonies should unite on an Iroquois model at the 1744 Lancaster Treaty. He interprets what Canassatego said as "bragging" to burnish the Iroquois Confederacy's image in the eyes of the English, not as political advice.

**1975.004.** Brotherston, Gordon. "The Prairie and Cooper's Invention of the West," in *James Fenimore Cooper: New Critical Essays*, Robert Clark, ed. Totowa, N.J.: Barnes & Noble Books, 1985, pp. 162-186.

> On page 169, Brotherston writes: "Just as the epithet 'fiendish' attaches to the Iroquois Confederacy which had in fact 'provided a wall of safety for the English colonies during 150 years of national adolescence,' and whose constitution served as a model for the United States itself, so from the start the Sioux are billed as 'demons,' 'devils,' 'reptiles,' and monstrously treacherous, although they had actually protected United States soldiers during their first incursions west of the Missouri-Mississippi." The quotation is from Paul Wallace, "Cooper's Indians," *New York History* 35(1954), p. 425.

**1975.005.** Campbell, Janet and David. "Cherokee Participation in the Political Impact of the North American Indian." *Journal of Cherokee Studies* 6:2(Fall, 1981), pp. 92-105.

> This article notes the linguistic connection of the Iroquois and the Cherokees, and traces Iroquoian influence on the founding of democracy in the new United States, citing Franklin's letter to James Parker (1751), Franklin's Articles of Confederation, and the bundle of arrows and eagle on the United States Great Seal.

**1975.006.** Chase, James S. [Review of Johansen, *Forgotten Founders* (1982)]. *History: Reviews of New Books* 11:8(July, 1983), p. 181.

> Chase, of the University of Arkansas, finds *Forgotten Founders* to be "graceful, appealing, and elegantly turned out." He says that Johansen is persuasive in arguing that Benjamin Franklin was familiar with, and admired the political structure of the

Iroquois Confederacy.  The book is less convincing, Chase writes, in establishing "the Iroquois as the principal source of Franklin's ideas."  Chase suggests that this book "will inspire a more rigorous exegesis of this fascinating subject."

**1975.007.** Deloria, Vine, Jr. and Clifford Lytle.  *American Indians, American Justice.* Austin: University of Texas Press, 1983.

> This legal history develops the idea of Iroquois influence on United States political development on page 82:  "It is interesting to note that the first written constitution in North America appeared before Columbus....The *Gayaneshagowa*, or Great Binding Law of the Five Nations, was a written constitution created by the Iroquois [which] enunciated such democratic ideas and doctrines as initiative, recall, referendum, and equal suffrage.  It provided the type of central government that would later be suggested by Benjamin Franklin to the colonies as an institution worthy of emulation....[T]he Iroquois Constitution provided a written preview of some of the governmental values later adopted by the whites in America."  Felix Cohen is cited as a source.

**1975.008.** Fenton, William N.  "Structure, Continuity, and Change in the Process of Iroquois Treaty Making," in Francis Jennings, ed.  *The History and Culture of Iroquois Diplomacy: An Interdisciplinary Guide to the Treaties of the Six Nations and Their League.*  Syracuse: Syracuse University Press, 1985.

> Page 29: "Then one may observe how Canassatego, the Onondaga...lectured the Colonials on the advantages of union [at the Lancaster Treaty Council, 1744]."

**1975.009.**  Graymont, Barbara.  [Review of Johansen, *Forgotten Founders* (1982)].  *New York History* 64:3(1983), pp. 325-327.

> Graymont finds *Forgotten Founders* to be "gracefully written and attractively printed" (p. 325), but too far-reaching in its assertion of Iroquois precedent for American democracy.  While Graymont does not think *Forgotten Founders* has "proved...conclusively" that the Iroquois were "the model" (her phrase) for American federalism, she says that the book raises "other interesting questions that should be pursued in more depth" (p. 325).  She is interested particularly in "what influence the examples of American Indian societies had on the

thinking of the *philosophes* and their concepts of natural rights and natural law."

**1975.010.** Jacobs, Wilbur. *Dispossessing the American Indian: Indians and Whites on the Colonial Frontier.* Norman: University of Oklahoma Press, 1985.

> Pages 168-170: "Academics still argue about whether the Indian confederations of colonial times had a tangible influence upon the fathers of the Constitution. The case for the Indians is not so far-fetched as one might think. Franklin, an admirer of the Iroquois League, had good reason to know its virtues for he had been an Indian commissioner at treaties, and....It is known that other framers of the Constitution had a knowledge of Indian confederation systems and the ideals of Indian democracy. Moreover, these statesmen were avid readers of the French *philosophes* whose writings were partly influenced by descriptions of North American Indians set forth in the writings of the French Jesuit missionaries. The noble savage idea, hammered into the writings of Michel de Montaigne and later French writers, including Rousseau, was embellished with the ideas of natural rights, the equality of man, and with the democratic tribal traditions of North American Indians."

**1975.011.** Johansen, Bruce E. *Forgotten Founders: Benjamin Franklin, the Iroquois and the Rationale for the American Revolution.* Ipswich, Mass.: Gambit, 1982.

> Reviews of *Forgotten Founders* appeared in *Choice* (March, 1983), University of Nebraska at Omaha *Gateway* (January 21, 1983 and June 24, 1983), University of Washington *Daily* (July 21, 1982), *The Atlantic* (February, 1983), The Los Angeles *Times* (December 21, 1982), University of Washington *Alumnus* (Winter, 1982), *New Age* (November, 1982), *Publishers Weekly* (February 5, 1982), *Booklist* (May 15, 1982), The Boston *Globe* (November 25, 1982), The St. Louis *Post-Dispatch* (December 5, 1982), *In These Times* (May 4, 1983), The Seattle *Times* (May 30, 1982), The Milwaukee *Sentinel* (March 4, 1983), The Omaha *World-Herald* (August 14, 1983) and *The Journal of Interdisciplinary History*, [n.d.]

> After it was published in the fall of 1982, *Forgotten Founders* was reviewed with an incredible diversity of reactions, including some impressive reviews in the trade press and some

large newspapers. Most academic journals initially ignored the book. At that time, the idea that American Indian political organization helped shape our own seemed to be a frontier outpost of mystery, myth, and rumor, far off their cognitive maps. A sampling of excerpts from the reviews illustrates their contrasts:

"Its editorializing and fragile logic render it passe."
   *--CHOICE*

(This unsigned review faulted Johansen for neglecting to reference Volume 15 of the *Handbook of American Indians*, which contains a lengthy piece by Elisabeth Tooker on the Iroquois League.)

"[*Forgotten Founders*] is the language of 20 years ago, of more idealistic times."
--"Whitcomb," University of Nebraska at Omaha *Gateway*

("Whitcomb" was a pen name of Joe Brennen, a UNO student and editor of the *Gateway*, who enjoyed posing as a hard-scrabble newspaper reporter twice his age. It was a positive review, despite this concluding sentence.)

"A stimulating and unexpected view of history."
*--The Atlantic*

"The Indians did indeed give us more than corn."
--Michael Parfit in the *Los Angeles Times Book Review*, December 21, 1982

"A refreshing and provocative view..."
*--New Age*

"A thoughtful venture into an area clearly in need of more research."
*--Publishers Weekly*, Feb. 5, 1982

"An intriguing little book, professionally conceived and executed..."
*--Booklist*, May 15, 1982

"If the Johansen book gets around, as it should, we'll be seeing a toast or two to the Iroquois next Fourth of July."
--Ray Murphy, Boston *Globe*

"Johansen...has assembled an imposing array of facts to support his findings."
--Carl R. Baldwin, St. Louis *Post-Dispatch*

"Perhaps the greatest hidden secret in all American history..."
--Harvey Wasserman, *In These Times*

"A most unusual and provocative study."
--Larry Rumley, Seattle *Times*

"One is never sure just how much is being claimed...the sources need to be used more critically to distinguish the mere rhetorical use of the 'noble savage' idea from the actual borrowing and influence that he seems to assert."
--Karen Ordahl Kupperman, *Journal of Interdisciplinary History*

"*Forgotten Founders* rests on a misconception, draws on limited research, and is written with small attention to the meaning of the sources it does use."
--Bernard W. Sheehan, Indiana University, *Journal of Interdisciplinary History*

"Although this is a book I wish I could praise....It reads like the dissertation it once was..."
--David Stineback, *American Indian Quarterly* (Spring, 1989)

**1975.012.** Katz, Jane B., ed. *This Song Remembers: Self-Portraits of Native Americans in the Arts.* Boston: Houghton-Mifflin Co., 1980.

On page 45, an editor's introduction of Peter Jemison briefly describes the use of consensus in Iroquois governance, adding: "This early form of democracy is believed by some to have set the pattern for the framers of the United States Constitution."

**1975.013.** Kincaid, J. "Toward the Third Century of American Federalism: New Dynamics and New Perspectives." *American Studies International* 22:1 (1984).

**1975.014.** Leacock, Eleanor. "Women's Status in Egalitarian Society: Implications for Social Evolution." *Current Anthropology,* June, 1978 (Vol. 19, No. 2), pp. 247-275.

Leacock discusses Iroquois society, with special attention to the works of Lewis Henry Morgan, on pp. 252-253.

**1975.015.** Lucas, Phil. "Images of Indians." *Four Winds: The International Forum for Native American Art, Literature, and History.* Autumn, 1980, pp. 68-77.

> In this survey of Native American images in film, Lucas discusses Native American contributions to American culture, among them "concepts of personal liberty and our democratic form of government itself." Lucas quotes to this effect from Felix Cohen's 1952 article in *The American Scholar.*

**1975.016.** Poatgieter, Hermina. *Indian Legacy: Native American Influences on World Life and Culture.* New York: Julian Messner/Simon & Schuster, 1981.

> This book for young people surveys Native American contributions to a number of aspects of everyday American life, including sports, agriculture, medicine, *et al.* The first chapter, entitled "Indian Influence on Government and Political Ideas," outlines interactions between Franklin and the Iroquois in some detail. It also develops ideas of freedom and liberty within a Native American context, quoting liberally from the writings of Thomas Jefferson. Much of this material is adapted from Felix Cohen's "Americanizing the White Man" (1952). Some of it may have come by way of Virgil Vogel, who uses them in his work *This Land Was Ours* (1972). Vogel read Poatgieter's manuscript and offered critical advice.

**1975.017.** Rosenblatt, Judith, ed. *Indians in Minnesota, 4th Ed.* [1962] Minneapolis, Minn.: University of Minnesota Press, 1985.

> The first page of the introduction (p. 3) of *Indians of Minnesota,* contains a salute to the Iroquois Confederacy, which "so impressed America's early statesmen that it became the model for the union of the colonies and the government of the United States...." This book cites Josephy, *America's Indian Heritage* (1968).

**1975.018.** Spence, Cathy. "Did the Indians Teach the Pilgrims Democracy? Yes, Says Manuscript Uncovered by Local Man -- and Therein Lies a Tale." North Shore (Mass.) *Weekly,* September 5, 1984.

> This newspaper article details the discovery by Dan Mahoney, a Boston resident, of an unpublished manuscript written by

William James Sidis during the 1930s, after Sidis vanished from the media limelight. The youngest person to graduate from Harvard, Sidis had been known as a fabulous prodigy, who could read five languages by the time he was five years of age. Fleeing media attention (stories on Sidis appeared on nineteen New York *Times* front pages), Sidis maintained in *Tribes and States* that the Penacook Indians of New England had been democratic, and had lent their institutions to immigrants from Europe. Sidis believed that the Penacooks had borrowed democratic institutions from the Iroquois.

**1975.019.** Suter, Coral and Marshall Croddy. "To Promote the General Welfare: the Purpose of Law." *Law in Social Studies Series.* Los Angeles, Calif.: Constitutional Rights Foundation, 1985.

This is a booklet designed for secondary-school students that attempts to infuse the study of law into history curricula. In Unit 1, "Law in a New World," students compare the consensual process used by the Iroquois with decisionmaking during the Salem witch trials.

**1975.020.** Todd, Lewis Paul and Merle Curti. *Triumph of the American Nation.* Orlando: Harcourt Brace Jovanovich, 1986.

This American history textbook is reported by Innerst (1988) to have said that "The example of the Iroquois Confederation had an influence on Benjamin Franklin and his efforts to promote an intercolonial union." The book makes that statement on page 50. On pp. 74-76, it briefly describes the Iroquois Confederacy's origins and organization.

**1975.021.** Williams, Robert A., Jr. "The Algebra of Federal Indian Law: The Hard Trail of Decolonizing and Americanizing the White Man's Indian Jurisprudence." *Wisconsin Law Review* (March, 1986), p. 219.

Williams supports his case for Native American self-governance by describing the Iroquois confederacy and its historic influence on the formation of the United States. He cites Canasatego's advice to colonial representatives in 1744, and Benjamin Franklin's 1751 letter to his printing partner James Parker, as well as Thomas Jefferson on Indian governance. He also cites Felix Cohen's 1952 essay in *The American Scholar.* Williams, a member of the Lumbee tribe, was visiting professor of law at the University of Arizona when this article was published.

**1975.022.** Wirt, Frederick M. [Review, Johansen, *Forgotten Founders*, 1982] *Publius: The Journal of Federalism*, Vol. 13, No. 3 (Summer, 1983).

**1975.023.** Vecsey, Christopher. "The Story and Structure of the Iroquois Confederacy." *Journal of the American Academy of Religion* 54:1(1986), pp. 79-106.

> In this outline of the Iroquois Confederacy's history and structure, Vecsey notes on p. 95 that "The Iroquois are probably influenced by U.S. and Canadian written laws, as these laws are possibly influenced by Iroquois concepts." *Forgotten Founders* (1982, 1987) is cited.

## Other Items

**1975.024.** Script, "Night of the First Americans," performed March 4, 1982 at the Kennedy Center for the Performing Arts, Washington, D.C. The script was written by Choctaw filmmaker Phil Lucas and included performances by a number of well-known Indian and non-Indian actors and artists, including Lorne Greene, Will Sampson, Jonathan Winters, Vincent Price, Paul Ortega, Ironeyes Cody, Martin Sheen, Dennis Weaver, Loretta Lynn, Dick Cavett, Hoyt Axton, Will Rogers, Jr., Kevin Locke, and Wayne Newton. The performance contained a substantial segment outlining the Iroquois role in the formulation of U.S. democracy. Lucas referenced working drafts of Johansen, *Forgotten Founders* (1982) for this material. Lucas and Johansen, both in Seattle at the time, were working together on the theme.

**1975.025.** Sound recording, Donald A. Grinde, Jr., "The Iroquois and the Origins of American Democracy," California State University at Sacramento Center for Instructional Media. This is an audio recording of a lecture given by Grinde in the university's visiting scholars' program, April 2, 1982.

# 1900 -1974

## *Books and Scholarly Journals*

**1900.001.** Armstrong, Virginia Irving. *I Have Spoken: American History Through the Voices of the Indians.* Chicago: Swallow Press, 1971.

> This collection of speech excerpts contains one (on page 42, item number 81) attributed to "a Cayuga chief" who "made an address before the New York Historical Society in 1808." This sentiment has been variously attributed to a number of sources during the nineteenth century, including Ely Parker. "Have we, the first holders of this region, no longer a share in your history? Glad were your fathers to sit down on the threshold of the Longhouse; rich did they hold themselves in getting the mere sweepings from the door."

**1900.002.** Barry, Richard. *Mr. Rutledge of South Carolina.* New York: Duell, Sloan and Pearce, 1942.

> Page 339: At the first meeting of the Drafting Committee (Committee of Detail) of the Constitutional Convention, John Rutledge, chairman of the committee "drew from his pocket a parchment, which had never been referred to in the convention or by any of its delegates outside, and read it aloud. It was a replica of the constitution of the Treaty of the Five Nations (the Iroquois) of 1520. Rutledge read what the Indians had written more than two and a half centuries before: 'We, the people, to form a union, to establish peace, equity and order.'" This unreferenced anecdote, which itself becomes a reference for a small number of other writers, is probably a fabrication. The Iroquois had no constitution written in a European-style language before the oral Great Law of Peace was committed to English in fragments beginning in the 1880s. A complete account was not published until 1992. The fabrication does contain an element of truth, however, in that the Iroquois had formed a union for peace, equity, and order.

**1900.003.** Beals, Katie and John J. Carusone. *Native Americans: The Constitution of the Iroquois League.* Oakland, Calif.: United School District, 1972.

This 53-page classroom guide developed by the Oakland Unified School District presents the political philosophy of the Iroquois League and ways in which Iroquois concepts were incorporated into the Constitution of the United States by the founders. The authors indicate that they developed this booklet to bring attention to the idea that the Iroquois helped shape United States political thought.

**1900.004.** Beauchamp, William M. *Civil, Religious, and Mourning Councils and Ceremonies* of *Adoption of the New York Indians.* New York State Museum Bulletin No. 113. Albany, N.Y.: New York State Education Department, June, 1907.

On page 342, while discussing the federal structure of the Iroquois Confederacy, Beauchamp writes that "Local affairs were left to national councils, as in our general and state governments." Beauchamp returns to the idea of Iroquois similarity to the United States political system on page 437, where he writes that "...the chiefs do not seem to have worn any distinctive badge....This is one of the curious resemblances in our national political system and that of the Iroquois. " Beauchamp attended several Iroquois political councils.

**1900.005.** Billard, Jules B., ed. *The World of the American Indian.* Washington, D.C.: National Geographic Society, 1974, 1979.

Page 133: "Our own nation's founding fathers knew of the Iroquois Confederacy, and admired its effectiveness. Wrote Benjamin Franklin: 'It would be a very strange Thing, if six Nations of ignorant Savages should be capable of forming a Scheme for such an Union.'"

**1900.006.** Brandon, William. "American Indians and American History." *The American West* 2:2(1965), pp. 14-25, 91-93.

Brandon devotes part of this article to Native American images of liberty in European imagination, including those images that helped inspire political revolution. On page 25, he writes: "Present, also, was the Indian, real or trans-substantial, in other storms of egalitarianism that subsequently swept the world." Brandon mentions the Tammany Society "which devoted itself to the cause of popular liberty and federal union..." Brandon also cites Frederich Engels' admiring description of the Iroquois polity (p. 91)

**1900.007.** Chamberlin, J. E. *The Harrowing of Eden: White Attitudes Toward Native Americans.* New York: Seabury Press, 1975.

> On page 136, Chamberlin observes that  "...[I]t is generally held that the model of the great Iroquois (Six Nations) Confederacy was a significant influence on both the Albany Plan [of 1754] and the later Articles of Confederation." In a footnote (pp. 227-28), Chamberlin also notes the Iroquois influence on Marx and Engels through Lewis Henry Morgan.

**1900.008.** Cohen, Felix. *Handbook of Federal Indian Law.* Albuquerque: University of New Mexico Press, 1942.

> On page 128, Cohen writes, regarding American Indians' ability to govern themselves: "Indeed, it may be said that the constitutional history of the Indian tribes covers a longer period and a wider range of variation than the constitutional history of the colonies, the states, and the United States. It was some time before the immigrant Columbus reached these shores, according to eminent historians, that the first federal Constitution on the American Continent was drafted, the *Gayaneshagowa*, or the Great Binding Law of the Five (later six) Nations (Iroquois). It was in this constitution that Americans first established the democratic principles of initiative, recall, referendum, and equal suffrage. In this constitution, also, were set forth the ideal[s] of the responsibility of governmental officials to the electorate, and the obligation of the present generation to future generations."

**1900.009.** Collier, John. *The Indians of the Americas.* New York: W. W. Norton, 1947, pp. 117-121.

> John Collier, Franklin D. Roosevelt's commissioner of Indian Affairs in the 1930s and 1940s, praised the Iroquois Confederacy as the most important Indian group in North America. Collier claimed that the Iroquois League was the greatest institutional achievement of humankind.  While emphasizing the practical aspects of its political organization, Collier thought of the Iroquois confederacy as an ideal democratic government which others should follow since it was a successful historical model. (pp. 117-121)

**1900.010.** Costo, Rupert and Jeannette Henry. *Textbooks and the American Indian.* San Francisco: Indian Historian Press, 1970.

> This critique of textbooks' treatment of American Indians faults them for ignoring "the influence of Native democratic thought and society" on"the developmental treatment of government in the United States." (p. 109). On page 124, this book faults *The United States Constitution in Perspective* (by Claude L. Heathcock, 1965) because "The influence of Indian philosophy and democratic thought upon the making of the Constitution is completely ignored." Again, on page 146, the authors write that all the books they have surveyed omit "the important facts of Indian influence upon and participation in government."

**1900.011.** Eckert, Allan W. *Wilderness Empire: A Narrative.* Boston: Little, Brown & Co., 1969.

> On page 624, Eckert writes: "The whites who were versed in politics at this time [the 1750s], had every reason to marvel at this [Iroquois] form of government. Knowledge of the League's success, it is believed, influenced the colonies in their own initial efforts to form a union, and later to write a Constitution."

**1900.012.** *Encyclopedia Britannica: A New Survey of Universal Knowledge.* Vol. 12. Chicago: University of Chicago, 1947.

> On p. 684, describing the Iroquois Confederacy's governing system: "In a sense, this was representative democracy." The entry ends by stating that "A shadow of the [Iroquois] League is still perpetuated as a ceremonial form."

**1900.013.** *Encyclopedia of Indians of the Americas.* St. Clair Shores, Mich.: Scholarly Press, 1974.

> This encyclopedia contains a timeline of Native American history that includes an item for 1754, "A plan of union among the colonies, drawn up by Benjamin Franklin and said to have been modeled after the Iroquois Confederacy was discussed at the Albany Congress." This material was reprinted in a curriculum utilized by the Philadelphia Urban Indian Center (United Indians of Delaware Valley) in 1997.

**1900.014.** Farb, Peter. *Man's Rise to Civilization as Shown by the Indians of North America From Primeval Times to the Coming of the Industrial State.* New York: E.P. Dutton & Co., 1968.

> On page 98, Farb observes that "The [Iroquois] League deeply impressed the white settlers, and some historians believe that it was one of the models on which the Constitution of the new United States was based. The League did somewhat resemble the union of the thirteen colonies in organization."

**1900.015.** Graymont, Barbara, ed. *Fighting Tuscarora: The Autobiography of Chief Clinton Rickard.* Syracuse, N.Y.: Syracuse University Press, 1973.

> On pages 131 and 132, Rickard recounts that in the late 1940s, after the United Nations was established, he was a member of Iroquois delegations which visited U.N. headquarters in New York City once a year, where "We brought our message of peace to the world body and reminded the delegates we met that we were the first United Nations."

**1900.016.** Hallowell, A. Irving. "The Backwash of the Frontier: The Impact of the Indian on American Culture," in Walker Wyman and Clifton Kroeber, eds., *The Frontier in Perspective.* Madison: University of Wisconsin Press, 1957.

> "It has been said that information about the organization and operation of the League of the Iroquois which Franklin picked up at various Indian councils suggested to him the pattern for the United States of America." (p. 232)

**1900.017.** Henry, Thomas R. *Wilderness Messiah: the Story of Hiawatha and the Iroquois.* New York: Bonanza Books, 1955.

> In this biography of Hiawatha, Henry quotes from the papers of J.N.B. Hewitt (which are housed at the Smithsonian Institution) and says that Hewitt "was firmly convinced that the League of the Iroquois was the intellectual progenitor of the United States." (p. 226)

**1900.018.** Jacobs, Paul and Saul Landau. *To Serve the Devil.* New York: Vintage Books, 1971, pp. 62-63. [See McLuhan, 1971, below]

**1900.019.** Jones, Louis Thomas. *Aboriginal American Oratory: The Tradition of Eloquence Among the Indians of the United States.* Los Angeles: Southwest Museum, 1965.

> On pages 115-116 of this book, Warcaziwin, "a full-blooded Sioux Indian woman," is said to have made a speech in 1930 at El Rancho Paso de Bartolo, a 16,000-acre estate once owned by Pio Pico, the last Mexican governor of California. Warcaziwin's speech began: "It is a sad commentary upon our American history to have to say that, to date, the American Indian does not occupy his just and sure place in America....Those from England, coming to the west, found a people having a very high form of government. It is to the...Iroquois Confederacy, that you owe, in a measure, many principles embodied in your Constitution." A footnote says that the address was recorded by a stenographer. A photograph of Warcaziwin is provided on p. 117.

**1900.020.** Kleiner, Jack. "United States Law on American Indians." *Case and Comment* 77:4(July / August, 1972): 3-4.

> Kleiner briefly describes the Iroquois political system and its similarity to the United States' structure. He also notes Iroquois symbols on the United States Great Seal, including the eagle and bundle of arrows.

**1900.021.** Kramer, Lucy. *Indians Yesterday and Today.* Washington, D.C.: Interior Department, 1941.

> Published six months before the United States entered World War II, this was one of a series of public-information booklets distributed by the Interior Department. This booklet, which was printed at the Chilocco (Oklahoma) Agricultural School, contains a final chapter by John Collier, commissioner of Indian affairs. On page 27, at the end of a chapter on Indian contributions to American civilization, this booklet contains a comment on the idea that the Iroquois helped shape American democracy: "Some students of ethnology hold that the very form of our Federal Government was built on the pattern of [the] Iroquois confederacy. Certain it is that the constitution of the Iroquois, which had been in existence for many years before the American Revolution, presented at once a model and a challenge to the English colonies of the New World. But that is a story in itself."

**1900.022.** Lindsay, J.O. ed. *The New Cambridge Modern History: the Old Regime, 1713-1763.* Cambridge: Cambridge University Press, 1970, vol. VII.

> On page 65, Lindsay observes the use to which "Montesquieu...made of a...noble savage to point a criticism of European conditions was an indication of how much the impact of other civilisations was affecting European ways of thought."

**1900.023.** Mathur, Mary E. *The Iroquois in Time and Space: A Native American Nationalistic Movement.* Ph.D. dissertation, University of Wisconsin, 1971.

> Mathur argues that Franklin's Albany Plan more closely resembled the Iroquois model than anything that British political society had to offer at the time.

**1900.024.** Mathur, Mary E. Fleming. "Tiyanoga of the Mohawks: Father of the United States," *Indian Historian,* 3:2(Spring, 1970), pp. 59-62,66.

> Mathur's article, possibly excerpted from her dissertation (above), is an early, and detailed, explication of Hendrick's role with British colonial leaders in advocating colonial union on an Iroquois model, especially at the Albany Congress of 1754. Regarding "the debt owed by the United States to the Iroquois," writes Mathur, Hendrick (Tiyanoga) "can be called the father of New York State and has an excellent claim to be the real father of the United States." (p. 64)

**1900.025.** McLuhan, T.C. *Touch the Earth: A Self-Portrait of Indian Existence.* New York: Outerbridge and Lazard, 1971.

> On page 100, this collection of Native American oratory republishes part of a paper, "Territorial Limits, Geographical Names and Trails of the Iroquois," which was read by Dr. Peter Wilson, a Cayuga, at a meeting of the New York Historical Society during 1847. Wilson said: "have we, the first holders of this prosperous region, no longer a share in your history. Glad were your fathers to sit upon the threshold of the Long House, rich did they hold themselves in getting the mere sweepings from its door." McLuhan's source for this quotation is: Lewis H. Morgan, *League of the Ho-de-no-sau-nee, or Iroquois.* New York: Dodd-Mead, 1904, Book 3, pp. 104-105.

The author adds that this quotation is also found in Paul Jacobs and Saul Landau, with Eve Pell, *To Serve the Devil*, chapter one ("The Indians"), in "Part 1," "Natives and Slaves," New York: Vintage Books, 1971, I:62-63.

**1900.026.** Moquin, Wayne, ed. *Great Documents in American Indian History.* New York: Praeger Publishers, 1973.

On page 159, with a reference to the 1901 edition of *League of the Haudenosaunee* by Lewis Henry Morgan (pp. 104-105), Moquin presents a statement that greatly resembles one that Armstrong (above) attributes to a Cayuga speaker in 1808. This one is attributed to Peter Wilson, a Cayuga, in May, 1847, in a speech to the New York Historical Society: "Have we, the first holders of this prosperous region, no longer a share in your history? Glad were your fathers to sit down on the threshold of the Long House. Had our forefathers spurned you from it, when the French were thundering at the opposite side to get a passage...and drive you into the sea, whatever has been the fate of other Indians, the Iroquois might still have been a nation, and I, instead of pleading here for the privilege of living within your borders, I -- might have had a country."

**1900.027.** Palmer, Rose. *The North American Indians: An Account of the American Indians North of Mexico, Compiled from the Original Sources.* Volume Four of the Smithsonian Scientific Series. [1929] Washington, D.C.: The Smithsonian Institution, 1934.

Palmer undertakes a detailed description of the Iroquois League, including its founding story and political organization. As part of this description, she writes, on page 81: "It was an extraordinary genius for social organization, which culminated in a confederation that endured through two centuries and in some respects served as a model for the union of the Colonies."

**1900.028.** Parker, Arthur C. "The Constitution of the Five Nations," in William N. Fenton, ed., *Parker on the Iroquois.* Syracuse: Syracuse University Press, 1968.

On page 11, Parker annotates his version of the Great Law of Peace with this statement: "Here, then, we find the right of popular nomination, the right of recall and of woman suffrage flourishing in the old America of the Red Man...centuries before it became the clamor of the new America of the white invader." Asks Parker: "Who now shall call the Indians and the Iroquois savages?"

**1900.029.** Reaman, G. Elmore. *The Trail of the Iroquois Indians: How the Iroquois Indians Saved Canada for the British Empire.* New York: Barnes & Noble, 1967.

> In his introduction, Reaman, an Englishman, reflects on Rudyard Kipling's poetic description, during the days of English empire, of "lesser breeds without the law." He then wonders how this description could ever be used to describe the Iroquois, a "race of people that could furnish the prototype of the Constitution of the United States...and whose confederacy has many of the aspects of the present-day United Nations." (p. xiv). Reaman also writes that "Socially, the Six Nations met the sociologist's test of higher cultures by giving a preferred status to women." (p. 24) He add that the Iroquois League "was a model social order in many ways superior to the white man's culture of the day....Its democratic form of government more nearly approached perfection than any that has been tried to date. It is claimed by many that the framers of the United States of America copied from these Iroquois practices in founding the government of the United States." (p. 27) This statement is drawn from a quote that is sourced by Reaman as "Duncan Campbell Scott, *Traditional History of the Confederacy of the Six Nations.* Prepared by a Committee of the Chiefs, Trans. by R. S. C., Section II, 1911, p. 12."

**1900.030.** Shorris, Earl. *The Death of the Great Spirit: An Elergy for the American Indian.* New York: New American Library, 1971.

> On page 101, Shorris writes: "...There is speculation that the form of government devised by Deganawidah and Hiawatha had some influence on the United States Constitution."

**1900.031.** Speck, Paul G. *The Iroquois: A Study in Cultural Evolution.* Bloomfield Hills, Mich.: Cranbrook Institute of Science, Bulletin #23, October, 1945.

> Speck, on page 26, finds the Iroquois "a decidedly democratic people." He quotes Clark Wissler (Volume I) regarding the likelihood that the Iroquois example helped shape attempts at federalism by Franklin.

**1900.032.** Van Doren, Carl. *Benjamin Franklin.* New York: The Viking Press, 1938.

> Van Doren notes Franklin's admiration of the Iroquois League's political system. He also suggests that Franklin's Albany Plan owes something to the Iroquois. Van Doren, on page 220, writes that Franklin found no model that suited his purposes in the Old World.

**1900.033.** Wallace, Paul A.W. "The Return of Hiawatha." *New York History* XXIX:4 (October, 1948), pp. 385-403.

> This is a published version of a paper that Wallace read to the annual meeting of the New York State Historical Association at Syracuse, New York, July 29, 1948. In this article, Wallace describes the founding of the Iroquois Confederacy and surveys conjecture regarding its founding date. Summarizing at the end, he asks "What value has a study of the ancient Five Nations have to us in the modern world?" He finds in the founding epic of the Haudenosaunee a story of how a group of people changed their collective behavior dealing with war and peace, and a reply to those who insisted that the new United Nations would fail because, they say, "You cannot abolish war because you cannot change human nature." Wallace says that the Iroquois example shows that "peace could be secured without wiping out nationalities and imposing...a super-state." Wallace also concludes that the Iroquois League can teach modern people how to preserve local autonomy in a larger confederation.

**1900.034.** Wallace, Paul A. W. "Cooper's Indians," in *James Fenimore Cooper: A Re-appraisal.* Cooperstown, N.Y.: New York State Historical Society, 1954.

> On page 59, Wallace writes: "This great people, the United Nations of the Iroquois, who called themselves Kanonsionni, 'the Longhouse,' (i.e. the United Household)...lived under an ancient constitution which they called the Great Law...whose confederacy provided Benjamin Franklin inspiration for his scheme of union." Wallace writes that Cooper misunderstood the Iroquois form of governance.

**1900.035.** Vogel, Virgil. *This Country Was Ours: A Documentary History of the American Indian.* New York: Harper & Row, 1972.

On page 48, Vogel quotes Lewis Henry Morgan: "The Iroquois commended to our forefathers a union of the colonies similar to their own as early as 1755." Later writers, writes Vogel, "have suggested that the Articles of Confederation, modeled after the earlier Albany Plan, were more influenced by the Iroquois model than any other." At this point, he references Matthew Stirling in the *National Geographic* (1937, above) and Felix Cohen's "Americanizing the White Man" (1952). Vogel then quotes Franklin's 1751 letter to James Parker urging confederation, invoking the Iroquois model.

## *Newspapers, Magazines, Pamphlets, and Newsletters*

**1900.036.** _____. *Puck*, May 16, 1914, n.p.

On May 16, 1914, only six years before the first national election in which women had the vote, *Puck*, a humor magazine, printed a line drawing of a group of Indian women observing Susan B. Anthony, Anne Howard Shaw and Elizabeth Cady Stanton leading a parade of women. A verse under the print read:

> *"Savagery to Civilization"*
>
> *We, the women of the Iroquois*
> *Own the Land, the Lodge, the Children*
> *Ours is the right to adoption, life or death;*
> *Ours is the right to raise up and depose chiefs;*
> *Ours is the right to representation in all councils;*
> *Ours is the right to make and abrogate treaties;*
> *Ours is the supervision over domestic and foreign*
> *        policies;*
> *Ours is the trusteeship of tribal property;*
> *Our lives are valued again as high as man's.*

**1900.037.** _____. Tulsa *Daily World*, July 31, 1949.

This newspaper account calls the League of the Iroquois "a sort of Magna Charta" and states that it "was perhaps the first constitutional government...in the New World." The report asserts that few Americans know how "...the workings of the league affected the thinking of the framers of our constitution."

**1900.038.** Akweks, Aren [Ray Fadden]. *The Creation.* Hogansburg, N.Y.: Akwesasne Mohawk Counselor Organization, 1948.

> This pamphlet, which describes the Iroquois creation story of life on Turtle Island, contains a dedication to "to our friend and faithful brother, Teg-wan-dah, or Dr. W. D. McFadden of Middleport, N.Y." McFadden, "a student and authority on the culture of and the history of the Ho-de-no-sau-nee," was adopted by the Tonawanda Senecas. He added a message to the introduction of this booklet, which reads, in part: "Benjamin Franklin's Plan for Union of the Thirteen Colonies was directly inspired by the wisdom, the durability, and the inherent strength which he observed in the Constitution of the Iroquois Indians."

**1900.039.** Jemison, Alice Lee. "Civilization and the Indians." Washington *Star*, April 4, 1932.

> Jemison writes: "To the council fires of our league [Jemison was Seneca], came the great of colonial times: Benjamin Franklin, Timothy Pickering, Gen. Lafayette and other only slightly less distinguished. [They] came not only to negotiate and treat with this recognized power, but to observe and study the methods whereby six distant nations or states, each with an independent internal government, were bound together and governed by a national council." Jemison quoted Senator William Borah of Idaho as saying that the government of the United States had no European foundation, but was established upon the basic principles of the League of the Iroquois.

**1900.040.** Stirling, Matthew W. "America's First Settlers, the Indians." *National Geographic Magazine*, 72:5 (1937).

> In 1937, Matthew W. Stirling, chief and later director of the Bureau of American Ethnology (1928-1958) stated in an article in the *National Geographic* that the Albany Plan of Union was greatly influenced by the League of the Iroquois. Page 535: "The organized confederacy of the Iroquoian tribes, with a representative form of government, was a unique experiment among American Indians. There is good evidence that the League of the Iroquois strongly influenced our own democratic form of government." He further stated, in the Washington *Post*, February 7, 1950, that the Iroquois had a profound impact

on the formation of the American state. Stirling reiterated his respect for American Indian ways when he stated that "perhaps we can learn the elusive secret to world-wide peace from [the Iroquois]."

## *Other Items*

**1900.041.** Mrs. Mildred F. Garlow, "Demarcation of the 5 Nation Confederic Democracy -- *Novus Ordo Seclorum*," August 10, 1959, in William N. Fenton Papers, Letterbox entitled: "Letters from the Iroquois," Manuscript #20, American Philosophical Society.
In 1959, Mrs. Mildred F. Garlow (Seneca Deer Clan Mother) raised the issue of the Iroquois roots of American democracy. Garlow recounted the origin of the League of the Iroquois and then stated that the concepts of democracy implemented in "...the United States deleted and infringed [upon Iroquois ideas] by being mingled with...Political Science." Garlow discounted Greek and Roman antecedents for American government and then asserted that "...the founding fathers... deleted the moral laws of democracy, creating an autocratic government." She further believed that the United States's founders "...camouflaged themselves [under] the outspread wings of the unique American bald eagle, the five pointed star, arrows and quiver, etc. by their political science with the emblem of the Iroquois....Democracy is cradled in the Longhouse of the Iroquois [and]...the government of the United States. Democracy did not come from the Eastern Hemisphere; it was not created in the Western Hemisphere by the Eastern Mind. It was in operation long before Christopher Columbus' time.

**1900.042.** Press Release, Smithsonian Institution, Thursday November 5, 1953, in William N. Fenton Papers, Manuscript #20, Box entitled: Correspondence relating to publications, 1935-1957, American Philosophical Society. The press release issued on November 5, 1953 stated: "The bald eagle, symbol of the American Republic, also was the over-all symbol of the Iroquois republic, the League of the Six Nations in New York State, which preceded it."

# 1800 - 1899

## *All Sources*

**1800.001.** _____. *Albany Law Journal.* 45:10 (March 5, 1892).

By the 1890s, women's property rights were beginning to change in states such as Mississippi, and in at least one case, this change was traced back half a century to the inspiration of the Chickasaws. A report in the *Albany Law Journal*, March 5, 1892, remarked that: "It is said, and it is no doubt true, that our first married woman's law 'in the statute of 1839' embodied and was suggested by the tribal customs of the Chickasaw Indians, who lived in our borders." (p. 199)

**1800.002.** _____. *New York Evening Post*, Sept. 24, 1875.

Writing about the Iroquois in The New York *Evening Post*, Matilda Joslyn Gage contended that "division of power between the sexes in this Indian republic was nearly equal."

**1800.003.** _____. "Onondaga Indians," *Harper's Weekly*, February 17, 1872.

Governor Horatio Seymour of New York (1853-1855) stated while in office that: "Government of the whole, by the whole and for the benefit of the whole are native here, and are no more to be traced back to the old world than are the granite rocks on which we stand."

**1800.004.** _____. [Untitled] Syracuse *Journal*, January 10, 1866.

An Iroquois chief, Peter Wilson, is reported to have remarked at a New York Historical Society meeting in 1866 that there should be "...universal suffrage, even of women, as in" the Six Nations. Wilson also asserted that the Iroquois created a republican government that 'Thomas Jefferson copied largely from their constitution."

**1800.005.** _____. "Indians of New York," Utica *Morning Herald*, May 9, 1894.

Hon. Elliot Danforth, former New York State treasurer, asserted before the Oneida Historical Society that "The five nations [Iroquois] were confederated in a barbarian republic upon the unique plan afterward adopted by our states and our national republic."

**1800.006.** Brownell, Charles de Wolf. *The Indian Races of America: A General View.* Boston: Dayton and Wentworth, 1855.

> In this survey of Native American cultures in the Western Hemisphere, Brownell writes, on page 287, that "The nature of the [Iroquois] league was decidedly democratic; arbitrary power was lodged in the hands of no ruler....A singular unanimity was generally observed in their councils." Brownell then adds, on the same page: "We are told that for a long period before the [American] revolution, the Iroquois chiefs and orators held up their own confederation was an example for the imitation of the English colonies." By whom Brownell is told this, he does not say. This book was reprinted in 1865 by Hurlbut-Scranton Publishers of Hartford, Conn. under the title *The Indian Races of North and South America.*

**1800.007.** Child, Lydia Maria. *History of the Condition of Women, in Various Ages and Nations,* [1835].

> While the landmark Seneca Falls conference, usually credited today with beginning the modern feminist movement in the United States, was not held until 1848, the ideological basis for the movement was set down by Lydia Maria Child in her *History of the Condition of Women, in Various Ages and Nations,* published in 1835. Child's book used the Iroquois and Huron cultures to counterpoise notions of European patriarchy, illustrating the importance of the woman's role in political decisionmaking.

**1800.008.** Clinton, De Witt. "A Discourse [on the Six Nations] Delivered Before the New York Historical Society, at their Anniversary Meeting, 6th December, 1811" (New York: Van Winkle and Wiley, 1814), p. 50 (Early American Imprints, Second series; no. 38779).

> Speaking before the New York Historical Society in 1811, De Witt Clinton (a member of the New York Tammany Society) stated that all of the proceedings of the Iroquois "...were conducted with great deliberation and were distinguished for order, decorum, and solemnity." *The New Yorker* also asserted that in "...eloquence, in dignity, and in all characteristics of profound policy, they surpassed an assembly of feudal barons, and were perhaps not far inferior to the great...Council of Greece." Clinton concluded that Native Americans have "...all

the indications of an incipient civilization." He also asserted that the Iroquois were "...the Romans of the Western World."

**1800.009.** Cralle, Richard K., ed., *The Works of John C. Calhoun.* New York: Appleton & Co., 1851, Vol. I, pp. 71-72.

John C. Calhoun, in his "Disquisition on Government and a Discourse on the Constitution and Government of the United States" stated that "governments of concurrent majority" were practical because the Iroquois utilized such a system. Calhoun believed that the "..federal, or general government..." of the "Six Nations" constituted a "council of union" in which each member possessed a veto on its decisions so that nothing could be done without the united consent of all. Instead of making the Confederacy weak, or impracticable, the veto had the opposite effect. It secured harmony, and with it a great increase of power. The Six Nations became the most powerful of all the Indian tribes within the limits of our country. They carried their conquest and authority far beyond the country they originally occupied, said Calhoun. who had dealt with the Iroquois as Secretary of War.

**1800.010.** Engels, Frederick. *Origin of the Family, Private Property, and the State, in Light of the Researches of Lewis Henry Morgan,* in *Selected Works.* London: Lawrence & Wishart, 1968, 3:201.

Having discovered the "mother-right gens," in the works of Lewis Henry Morgan on the Iroquois, Engels could scarcely contain himself: "It has the same significance for the history of primitive society as Charles Darwin's theory of evolution has for biology, and Marx's theory of surplus value for political economy...*The mother-right gens has become the pivot around which this entire science* [political economy] *turns.*" [emphasis added]

**1800.011.** Gage, Matilda Joslyn. *Woman, Church and State,* [1893] Watertown, Mass.: Peresphone Press, 1980.

Gage's *Woman, Church and State* [1893] on page 10 acknowledges that the modern world [is] indebted to the Iroquois "for its first conception of inherent rights, natural equality of condition, and the establishment of a civilized government upon this basis." Gage was probably one of the three most influential feminist architects of the nineteenth-century women's movement, with Elizabeth Cady Stanton and Susan B. Anthony. Gage was later "read out" of the movement and its history because of her radical views, especially regarding oppression of women by organized religion. Gage opened the book with a chapter on "The Matriarchate," a form of society she believed existed in a number of early societies, specifically the Iroquois. Gage discussed several Iroquois traditions that tended to create checks and balances between the sexes, including descent through the female line, the ability of women to nominate male leaders, the fact that women had a veto power over decisions to go to war, and the woman's supreme authority in the household. Gage also noted that Iroquois women had rights to their property and children after divorce. Gage also cited a statement by Hon. George Bancroft (p. 11) asserting that the United States borrowed some of its forms of government from the Six Nations. Gage herself was admitted to the Iroquois Council of Matrons, and was adopted into the Wolf Clan, with the name *Karonienhawi,* "she who holds the sky." "Never was justice more perfect, never civilization higher than under the Matriarchate," Gage wrote. (p. 9) "Under [Iroquois] women the science of government reached the highest form known to the world," Gage believed. (p. 10)

**1800.012.** Griffis, William E. *Sir William Johnson and the Six Nations.* New York: Dodd, Mead & Co., 1891.

On pages 53 and 54, Griffis advises further study of Iroquoian influence on the formation of the United States, especially Benjamin Franklin's role.

**1800.013.** Johnson, E. Pauline. "The Iroquois of Grand River." *Harper's Weekly,* June 23, 1894. [http://www.humanities.mcmaster.ca/~pjohnson/h5grad.html]

In a profile of the Grand River Iroquois reserve in Ontario, the noted Mohawk poet E. Pauline Johnson describes the Iroquois polity in the words of her contemporary, ethnologist Horatio Hale: "The laws and policy framed by Hiawatha and his associates more than four centuries ago are still in force among their descendants in this district. In this small domain the chiefs are still elected. The councils are still conducted and the civil policy is decided as nearly as possible by the rules of their ancient league. Not many persons are aware that there exists in the heart of Canada this relic of the oldest constitutional government of America -- a free commonwealth older even than any in Europe except those of England and Switzerland, and perhaps two small semi-independent republics which lurk in the fastnesses of the Pyrenees and the Apennines."

**1800.014.** Marx, Karl and Frederick Engels, *Selected Works*. New York: New World Paperbacks, 1968. p. 528. [citing Frederick Engels in 1886].

Engels described Iroquois society from his study of Lewis Henry Morgan's works: "Everything runs smoothly without soldiers, gendarmes, or police; without nobles, kings, governors, prefects, or judges; prisons, without trials. All quarrels and disputes are settled by the whole body of those concerned...not a bit of our extensive and complicated machinery of administration is required...There are no poor and needy...All are free and equal, including the women." (p. 528)

**1800.015.** Morgan, Lewis Henry [a.k.a. Skenandoah]. "Letters on the Iroquois." *The American Review: A Whig Journal* 26 (February, 1847), pp. 180-181.

Morgan notes that "The people of the Longhouse commended to our ancestors a union of the colonies similar to their own as early as 1755," possibly a reference to the Albany Plan of Union, authored by Benjamin Franklin, although, apparently unknown to Morgan, the Iroquois sachem Canassatego had urged the colonists to unite on the Iroquois model as early as 1744. Morgan believed that the Iroquois saw in the colonies "the common interests and common speech...the elements for a confederation."

**1800.016.** Morgan, Lewis Henry. *League of the Haudenosaunee, or Iroquois*. [1851] New York: Dodd, Mead & Co., 1922.

Nearly a century after the pivotal events that formed the United States, Morgan characterized the Iroquois League as a federal model very much like the new nation: "The nations [of the Iroquois League] sustained nearly the same relation to the league that the American states bear to the Union. In the former, several oligarchies are combined within one, in the same manner as [in] the latter, several republics are embraced in one republic." (p. 3)

**1800.017.** Morgan, Lewis Henry. *Ancient Society.* New York: Henry Holt & Co, 1877.

> It was Morgan's view that the Iroquois Confederacy "contained the germ of modern parliament, congress and legislature." (p. 119)

**1800.018.** Parker, Ely S. "Address to the New York State Historical Society, May 27, 1847," in Ely S. Parker Papers, Reel 1, American Philosophical Society.

> In this speech, the Seneca Ely S. Parker noted that the Iroquois had lost their land and were still losing it. Parker noted that in the Iroquois treaties of the 18th century, the Iroquois were "...one in council with you and...one in interest." Speaking of the fascination of the founding fathers with the Iroquois League, Parker finally noted that "Glad were your forefathers to sit upon the thresholds of the Longhouse[;] rich did they hold themselves in getting the mere sweepings from its door." Parker was secretary to U.S. Grant during the Civil War, and, once Grant became president, was appointed to serve as commissioner of Indian affairs, the first Native American to hold that office.

**1800.019.** "The Six Nations," in *Encyclopedia Americana* (1896), XIV (copy in J. N. B. Hewitt Papers, NAA, Smithsonian Institution).

> At the beginning of the Twentieth Century, the "Six Nations" article in the *Encyclopedia Americana* would state that the founders "in framing a Constitution for the United States, honored these people by the adoption of their general constitutional system."

**1800.020.** Stanton, Elizabeth Cady. "The Matriarchate or Mother-age," [address before the National Council of Women, February, 1891], *The National Bulletin,* Vol. 1, No. 5, (February, 1891).

> Elizabeth Cady Stanton referred to Lewis Henry Morgan's work in her address to the National Council of Women in 1891. Stanton referred to the influence of Iroquois women in national councils, and to the fact that their society was descended through the female line, and (like Gage), to the irony that

"our barbarian ancestors seem to have had a higher degree of
justice to women than American men in the 19th century,
professing to believe, as they do, in our republican principles of
government." Stanton surveyed the research of Morgan and
others which indicated that "Among the greater number of the
American aborigines, the descent of property and children were
in the female line. Women sat in the councils of war and peace
and their opinions had equal weight on all questions." (p. 1) In
this regard, she mentioned the Iroquois' councils specifically.
(p. 1) After surveying tribal societies in other parts of the
world as well, Stanton closed her speech with a case for sexual
equality: "In closing, I would say that every woman present
must have a new sense of dignity and self respect, feeling that
our mothers, during long periods in the long past, have been the
ruling power and that they used that power for the best
interests of humanity. As history is said to repeat itself, we
have every reason to believe that our turn will come again[.] It
may not be for woman's supremacy, but for, the as yet untried
experiment of complete equality, when the united thought of
man and woman will inaugurate a just government, a pure
religion, a happy home, a civilization at last in which
ignorance, poverty and crime will exist no more. Those who
watch already behold the dawn of the new day." (p. 7)

# Subject Index

# Author Index

**About the Compiler**

BRUCE E. JOHANSEN is Robert T. Reilly Professor of Communication and Native American Studies at the University of Nebraska. He has written twelve books on Native American topics, including recently *The Encyclopedia of Native American Legal Tradition* (Greenwood, 1998) and *The Encyclopedia of Native American Economic History* (Greenwood, 1999).

www.ingramcontent.com/pod-product-compliance
Lightning Source LLC
Chambersburg PA
CBHW061923020426
42338CB00003B/625